AD\
of WOMEN
ENTREPRENEURS

stories that inspire

ROBIN BEHRSTOCK
WITH DENNIS LOWERY
& CONTRIBUTION BY:

LORI AMES
STACEY BLUME
JENNY DORSEY
CARRIE HAMMER
JODY HARRIS
CYNTHIA JAMIN

ERIN JANKLOW
ERICKA MICHELLE LASSAIR
IRINA SKOERIES
MEREDITH SORENSEN
STEPHANIE WINANS
DAN CALDWELL

ADVENTURES *of* WOMEN ENTREPRENEURS

stories that inspire

RADIUS PRESS

ADVENTURES OF WOMEN ENTREPRENEURS
STORIES THAT INSPIRE
ROBIN BEHRSTOCK
WITH DENNIS LOWERY
CONTRIBUTORS:

LORI AMES	ERIN JANKLOW
STACEY BLUME	ERICKA MICHELLE LASSAIR
JENNY DORSEY	IRINA SKOERIES
CARRIE HAMMER	MEREDITH SORENSEN
JODY HARRIS	STEPHANIE WINANS
CYNTHIA JAMIN	DAN CALDWELL

Copyright © 2017. All rights reserved. No part of this book may be reproduced or transmitted in any form or by any means, electronic or mechanical, including photocopying, recording or by any information storage and retrieval system, without written permission from the author, except for brief quotations as would be used in a review.

ISBN 978-0-9987870-0-8 (TRADE PAPERBACK)

PUBLISHED BY RADIUS PARTNERSHIP LLC UNDER ITS RADIUS PRESS IMPRINT
PUBLISHED IN THE UNITED STATES OF AMERICA
DENVER, COLORADO

All statements of fact, opinion, or analysis expressed are those of the author and contributors and do not reflect the official positions or views of the publisher. Nothing in the contents should be construed as asserting or implying authentication of information or endorsement of the author's views. This book and subjects discussed herein are designed to provide the author's opinion about the subject matter covered and is for informational purposes only.

All images and pictures are used courtesy of the author or contributor unless otherwise captioned with credit.

TABLE OF CONTENTS

DEDICATION & ACKNOWLEDGMENTS

INTRODUCTION

ROBIN BEHRSTOCK, PART I..	1
LORI AMES: Necessity Can Pave the Way to Entrepreneurship...	21
STACEY BLUME: Making Something Utilitarian Fashionable...	31
JENNY DORSEY: It's Your Life... Own It..	48
CARRIE HAMMER: Creating the Brand That Changed an Industry...	66
JODY HARRIS: Strength Can Come from Adversity and Difficult Beginnings...	79
CYNTHIA JAMIN: Leaving a Dark Past Behind to Create a Bright Present and Future..	98
ERIN JANKLOW: The Importance of Authenticity.....................	120
ERICKA MICHELLE LASSAIR: Tearing Down to Rebuild and Restart Can Lead to Success...	140
IRINA SKOERIES: A Debilitating Disease Leads to a Healthy New Business...	155
MEREDITH SORENSEN: Everything You Do, Every Step You Take, Is What Makes You Who You Are........................	174
STEPHANIE WINANS: The Un-Sexy Entrepreneur.....................	191
DAN CALDWELL: Pushing Through Barriers.............................	202
ROBIN BEHRSTOCK, PART II..	224
AFTERWORD..	243
ABOUT THE AUTHOR..	251

DEDICATION & ACKNOWLEDGMENTS

This book is dedicated to all the entrepreneurs who took control of their destiny, created something special and made a positive impact on our society. They turned their dreams into reality, and are now inspirations to all future entrepreneurs whose stories have yet to be written.

Words cannot express the gratitude I feel for my family and their unconditional love and support. My parents, Andrea and Bruce, and sisters, Ellen and Alissa, have made me the person I am today, and I can't imagine where I'd be without them.

Thanks to my amazing friends Heidi, Julie, Jenny, Kristan, Corey and Matilda for their suggestions and advice along this literary journey. And thanks to my dog, Maggie, for always being by my side and making me smile every time she wiggles her butt.

Thank you also to the remarkable contributors and Dennis for your hard work, dedication and enthusiasm in being part of this project.

INTRODUCTION

This book is a compilation of stories from entrepreneurs meant to inspire people around the world to step outside their comfort zone, follow their passion and make their dreams a reality. The people featured are easy to relate to, all from different backgrounds, and followed different paths to entrepreneurship.

Many people want to achieve independence by creating a sustainable business that aligns with their passion. We hope this book shows that this aspiration is within everyone's reach, despite the challenges and barriers that might be in the way.

Aptly titled—its focus clear—why does it include a man's story? We saw it as an opportunity to be inclusive to all, and that it was an important tale to share about common challenges most entrepreneurs face at some time in their lives and business careers: BARRIERS. There are usually two components to them:

1) External – financial, educational, even cultural.
2) Internal – finding the right path to take, self-doubt and fear.

The second—internal—is the most significant to manage. If you can't then it's very hard, virtually impossible, to push through the external barriers. Perhaps the toughest obstacle is finding the right path to follow, and it sometimes can take several tries to find the right one. That is often the most important yet overlooked part of starting a successful entrepreneurial journey. Some entrepreneurs are trailblazers, breaking new ground and introducing new products and concepts to the world. But far more follow in already proven footsteps, and choosing the right ones—something you are passionate about and believe in—is what creates sustainable businesses. For many, that is the key to reaching their dreams.

ROBIN BEHRSTOCK

PART I

"Define success on your own terms, achieve it by your own rules, and build a life you're proud to live."
—ANNE SWEENEY, PRESIDENT OF WALT DISNEY

It was the 16th day of my six-month road trip, and I was rolling down a Wyoming highway in my Winnebago RV with my dog, Maggie, curled up in the passenger seat next to me. The plan was to drive across western North America, visiting customers and marketing my products. Much of the trip would be a solo journey, but friends would join for short segments, and I looked forward to meeting new people along the way. Miles and miles passed, and I enjoyed the solitude and life on the road.

That particular day I was listening to a Freakonomics podcasts, to men speaking about how to be great. My thoughts had been wandering as I listened. How do these people know what being great means? I started listening closer to the podcast, thinking at some point a woman would be included in the discussion. Much of what these men talked about seemed to tie back into one thing: to be great, you had to be the best at something.

That struck me, and I reflected on my experiences in life and business and my personal search to find fulfillment. I had learned that it is possible to create a great business and a great life by providing an excellent service or product that people need or want. And I discovered there are many different ways to 'be great.' I had also learned that it takes trial and error to get to that point, and you can reach it in relatively simple ways. Maybe 'being great' is opening a local coffee shop, serving fresh coffee and delicious baked muffins to people every day, getting to know the community, making friends and becoming a part of their daily ritual. That type of business might not make you financially rich, but it can make you feel accomplished and happy. You may not be Starbucks, but you built a great coffee shop that hundreds of neighbors can enjoy every day! The same could be said, and done, for some personal service type businesses, where your goal is to help people and make their day better in some way. Like so many things in life, success and 'greatness' is relative. A half empty glass may be half full. What feels like not enough to some, may be more than others have ever dreamed of having.

Life is about how we deal with circumstances and events. As women in the workforce, we often try to keep our footing on an uneven playing field. There are times when if it isn't pouring down rain, then the wind is blowing us sideways. One day we are on fire at our job, and other days work seems bitter cold. It is the contrast that allows us to love and appreciate the days when everything is flowing fine and beautiful both in our careers and our personal lives. The highs and lows of life are all relative and are learning opportunities. We must think differently about what success means, and how we can achieve contentment by finding it.

We—all human beings—are on a journey. I know that is a cliché, but it's true nonetheless. And sometimes we figure things out at unexpected points along the way.

For me, happiness and personal freedom are as important to consider as a measurement of success as skyrocketing revenue, profits and accumulating material possessions. Your own measure of success could be more about finding and doing what makes you happy and not so much about ego satisfaction or impressing others.

> *"Success is not the key to happiness. Happiness is the key to success. If you love what you are doing, you will be successful."*
> —Albert Schweitzer

When we set our own metric for what is meaningful and significant—and not merely follow what others say is the benchmark of success—we reach a crucial 'freedom point' in life as an entrepreneur. This holds true in personal life, too... but that's a whole other story. We become free from the fear of failure. We can be bold and not dread the outcome. Many experienced inventors rejoice at failed experiments because they know that means they are one step closer to success.

> *"Life is inherently risky. There is only one big risk you should avoid at all costs and that is the risk of doing nothing."*
> —Denis Waitley

I don't pretend to be the most courageous person in the world, but I do know that to get anywhere you must step out of your comfort zone. You can get pizza and other fast food delivered to you, but no one is going to pull into your driveway or parking lot, ring your door and say "here's that wonderful life you ordered." Okay! Great! Here's a twenty, keep the change!

True courage is doing what you need to do despite how hard or terrifying it might be. That's what drove me, and because of that inner push I achieved the life I've always wanted. Now, I was doing something extraordinary all because I kept trying and eventually found what was successful for me. I was rolling down the highway in my Winnebago RV, thinking about what I had accomplished and how telling others about it could be an inspiration to them.

Half, maybe two-thirds of the way to Missoula, in the historic town of Deer Park, I pulled off the interstate. I found a place to park and turned off the ignition switch. In the quiet, listening to the ticking of the cooling engine, at that moment I made the decision. Sitting there in some random parking lot, I started writing. After a while, I got back on the road but—as I drove—in my mind, I was already forming more of what I wanted to write about and the story to tell.

Four months later I had 28 pages of journaling and some great stories of life on the road while running my business. And more importantly, I had come to a realization and made a momentous decision to put my business up for sale. And then sold it to a private equity firm. All while on the road doing something I'd dreamed of doing for years! During that time, I had also parked my RV for a few days in Los Angeles and flown to Seattle to attend a women's entrepreneurship conference at Amazon. One of the speakers, Marla Beck, Founder of Blue Mercury, talked about her entrepreneurial journey; growing her business from one small location to a nationwide brand, and eventually selling it to Macy's, all while raising three small children. She ended her speech with something like this: "We often hear about all the great male entrepreneurs of the world, but we rarely hear stories about the great women. Keep on doing what you're doing, and maybe someday there'll be a book about us."

    I heard that and got chills up and down my spine; the good kind. I realized that my book—the one you're holding in your hands—shouldn't be just about me, but also other women entrepreneurs, their adventures, and inspiring stories. The words of Benjamin Franklin, too, echoed in my mind, "Write something worth reading, or do something worth writing." So, a plan had formed to find women entrepreneurs who had done things worth reading. To hopefully inspire readers to do something worth writing about and follow their dreams with passion!

    To have something worth sharing—a good story to tell—you must be willing to take a chance and do something new. I encourage you to get outside of your comfort zone, travel somewhere solo, learn a new language or a new hobby or try something you've always thought you never could. Maybe you just need a fresh challenge, or perhaps it's because you can no longer tolerate things, what was once merely uncomfortable has become unbearable. Whatever the case may be, it can become a catalyst to make a change and move toward a life where you feel fulfilled and happy.

> *"If you want something you've never had, you have to be willing to do something you've never done."*
> —Thomas Jefferson

A Bit of My Story

I had a pretty average, some would say privileged, childhood in a suburb of Chicago. Things changed when my parents decided to divorce my senior year in high school, and I ended up in the middle of a mess of accusations and constant fighting. I escaped the family drama by studying abroad three times and found comfort in my independence on the other side of the world. By the time the actual divorce was final, the fighting had gone on for 12 years. My mother, who had been a hard-working housewife for 25 years, went back into the workforce and found a full-time job to support herself. Her work ethic and tenacity inspired me to work hard and make enough money so I would never have to rely on anyone else to support me financially.

At an early age, my parents taught me about budgeting. I was given an allowance: $20/week. I had to learn to budget so I could pay for lunch at school all week and if there was money leftover, I could get ice cream or buy a slap bracelet. If I made my own lunch in the morning, then I wouldn't need to buy lunch at school and would have even more money left over for fun stuff. I could earn bonuses by doing extra chores and by getting A's on my report card.

My mom had a penchant for always telling my siblings and me that we were the best. As much as I rolled my eyes at the time, looking back, I'm grateful. Her kind and inspirational words instilled in me a measure of confidence that made me comfortable trying new things and not be afraid to fail. She was supportive, demanding without being pushy, and that is truly a great environment for a kid to excel. She also always reminded me to work hard and be nice. I believe the combination of self-assurance, hard work and being a good person has been a huge influence on my entrepreneurial journey. Thanks, Mom!

My parents had sold our house with the divorce, so every break from college I wondered where I would go. I loved Colorado and had made friends that I could stay with during those breaks, and found temporary jobs as a holiday helper at Vail Ski Resort. Staying continually busy throughout college and my young adult life didn't leave time for deep thoughts or reflections. Despite always being spread thin with plans, friends, sports and commitments, I would say, "Yes" to every invitation. I liked being busy and got excited at the prospect of meeting new people, going to new places and having new experiences. I would run from one activity to the next. It took some time for me to realize that was my way of continuing to ignore and repress my emotions. That pace—whether voluntary or involuntary—kept things at a superficial level.

Then in my mid- to late 20s I let myself get in deeper with someone than I ever had before. It didn't take long for me to feel like I was suffocating. Emotional conversations made me uncomfortable, and when pressed too hard they made me want to go into a dark room, alone and curl up in a ball. Emotional commitments scared me. All I wanted was to be independent and free.

These experiences had a great deal to do with my motivation to become an entrepreneur. Achieving success in business could be the ticket, it would be the means to a life of independence and self-sufficiency.

That being said, I had a lot to learn about the realities of business responsibilities, but that comes later in my story. They say 'entrepreneurs often work 80 hours a week to avoid working 40' and long hours no doubt were a part of the equation. I worked hard to save money and start an e-commerce business that I could manage at flexible times and from anywhere.

An Entrepreneur's Evolution

"The master has failed more times than the beginner has even tried."
—Stephen McCranie

Though I always felt I had an entrepreneurial spirit, that didn't exempt me from business failure. In college, I met a woman while interning with a company in London who made 'spec-traps,' which are nice looking pins that also hold reading glasses. I thought it was a great concept—think of how many people wear glasses—that market could be huge! I bought some stock from her and tried selling them to eyeglass stores when I returned to America. I made a few sales, but was busy with my studies and soon realized it wasn't the best product because the weight of the eyeglasses would eventually cause the pin to tear a hole in your shirt.

Other ideas seemed to fade with the wind. I met a guy whose company manufactured disposable breathalyzer tests. I thought everyone should have these in their car or purse. Why don't we see them at every gas station? I offered to help them distribute to new stores in exchange for a commission. They agreed to it, but for some reason, the idea fizzled.

I didn't know it then but understand fully now: most successful entrepreneurs worked their way through many things—business ideas and/or product iterations—to discover or find the one that takes off, and succeeds in the market.

> *"It is impossible to live without failing at something unless you live so cautiously that you might as well not have lived at all, in which case you have failed by default."*
> —J. K. Rowling

While working on these business ideas, I had a full-time position with a real estate development company. They sent me to an SEO (Search Engine Optimization) training class so I could help market their projects. I would be their resident 'SEO expert' and advise the rest of the marketing and development team. That went well, we had success marketing their projects, but then the market crashed, and I got laid off.

My former boss introduced me to his friend who imported hunting accessories. I began working for him and learned about manufacturing overseas, shipping, warehousing, and distribution. These were all the requirements—a perfect combination of experience and knowledge—to build my own brand of products to sell online.

While sourcing hunting accessories for my day job, I came across a factory that had a prototype for a bamboo Bluetooth keyboard. What a great idea, so many people want less plastic in their lives! Environmentally friendly electronics could be a great niche.

I worked with a designer to create the branding and attractive packaging and imported 100 bamboo keyboards. They sold well, and I decided to do a Kickstarter campaign to raise money for the next round of production. We reached our goal, raised over $26,000, and that enabled me to also work on adding new products to the line. We were making sales, but not enough for me to quit my day job.

Then there were issues with bamboo. It wasn't the most stable material, and it warped slightly with changes in the environment. A key would stick, and the keyboard became trash. Our product had 108 keys with 432 potentially stickable sides. That is a lot of potential for problems, which turned into reality. Our return rate was too high, and the only way we could make the product better was to use more plastic and less bamboo—decreasing the appeal of the product—which was not what we wanted to do. I kept my job and learned that next time I would keep the products simple, with as few potential problems as possible.

Most entrepreneurs remember the day when a 'golden business idea' comes to mind. Mine came one day in Vail, Colorado, summer of 2012, but the idea wasn't gold, it was copper. I was walking through town and decided to visit my friend Wes who worked at a classy bar called Up the Creek. I went inside for a drink and their liquor rep, Koren, came in soon behind me. She brought with her a box of copper mugs emblazoned with the Tito's Vodka logo. Everyone who worked at the bar gathered around to look at them. They told me what they were used for and recommended I try one, so I did. I ordered my first Moscow Mule, a cocktail made with vodka, ginger beer, and lime, served in one of the new copper mugs.

The drink was delicious but the way that frosty copper mug felt in my hands, the workmanship and tactile sense of just drinking from it... was so cool! Many more restaurants and bars could be using copper mugs, and people could have them at home, too! How fun would it be to entertain family and friends, serving them delicious drinks in beautiful copper mugs? So much potential, ding ding ding!

While sitting there at the bar, sipping my Moscow Mule, I did some research on my smartphone. Only two small businesses sold copper mugs online at the time. Now, here is where things converged for me, and I'm not the only entrepreneur who has experienced it. This was a great opportunity, but more importantly because of what I had learned from past jobs and experiences, I was better equipped to act on it. Also—and this is critical—I didn't tell myself, 'I'll check that out later.' I did it right then and there.

I bought the domain CustomCopperMugs.com on my smartphone at the bar that day. Then I posted a message in an import/export group on LinkedIn asking about manufacturers of copper mugs. One guy who responded from India, Ajay, seemed like he could be a good supplier and had competitive pricing.

I ordered samples, hired a photographer to take some product photos and built a simple website. The first product was a hundred mugs with a logo, and production would take 60 days. I only placed orders with the factory if I had an order from a customer. No risk, and no investment needed.

Then I decided to order a hundred blank mugs and sell them on Amazon. They sold within days! So, I ordered more and started adding different sizes, shapes, hammered finishes, antique finishes, etc., anything people were interested in buying. I moved as quickly as possible because even though things were going great, I knew that competition was inevitable. I didn't have time to spend on fancy packaging or branded inserts, just white boxes, and a white paper insert would do. And they did!

I decided to go to India to meet Ajay and see where the mugs were produced. I learned that he was actually a middleman. Some people think working with an intermediary is a bad thing, but Ajay has been a huge part of my business's success. When the first factory couldn't handle the increased volume, he got a second factory up and running without me having to lift a finger. When I had new products in mind that used other materials besides copper, he recommended other factories that would be a better fit for the particular product. However, after the first visit, I insisted on working directly with the factories. This did not mean I was cutting Ajay out of the picture. He would oversee the operations in India and act as the quality control department.

My company was originally called Custom Copper Mugs, but as it grew, most items were not custom, and we were doing a lot more than just copper mugs. I asked three creative friends to join me for margaritas, and we had a great brainstorming session to come up with a new company name. We wrote down words related to metals, drinkware, housewares... somehow that led to alchemy... handmade.... and then it came to us: Alchemade!

The domain name www.Alchemade.com was available, and the decision was made. I didn't want to lose the appeal of the original name which was very specific to our best-selling product, so I kept the old website and built another site with the new name.

Building a website may sound like a huge endeavor, but it's really not. If you can make a PowerPoint presentation, you can create a website. There are many templates available that are a great way to start. Then add high-quality photography, graphics, and text, and you are 95% of the way done. If you need additional customization beyond the template, a website developer can help. There are many options to find freelance website designers and developers at www.Upwork.com.

With the new website completed, I dove into marketing my products and chose Amazon as a prime venue. People often ask me if it's difficult to get started on Amazon. It is not! As long as you have product descriptions and product photography ready, it takes less than one hour to get an account up and running and list the first item.

Amazon is a very competitive marketplace, and there are programs that sellers can use to see what products are trending. Other retailers soon realized that copper mugs had become very popular and my competition grew quickly. I continually expanded my product lines with different sizes, styles, and finishes, and then added new products like shot glasses, shakers, punch bowls, ladles, trays, mint julep cups and more.

I marketed the custom logo'd copper mugs as promotional products to companies around the globe, and the business-to-business side of my operations grew. However, we had a large minimum order of one hundred pieces and a long lead time (60 days). Many customers didn't have enough time or wanted just a few custom mugs, and they were willing to pay a premium for it. I had to come up with a local solution for personalized mugs. I looked into engraving machine options, but the cost was around $20,000, which I was not comfortable spending. Instead, I did some research and found a man in Wisconsin with an engraving business, and we came to an agreement. I sent him boxes of blank mugs and about twice a week I sent him PowerPoint files with the details of each custom order. He completed the orders and shipped them to the customers. It worked okay, but there was no way for me to do any quality control since the orders were sent by the engraver. Unfortunately, there were lots of mistakes, orders sent to the wrong customers, etc. It seemed like the extra money we made on these custom mugs was not worth the customer service hassles.

However, about six months later, I got a call from the engraving machine company letting me know they were having a big sale. The $20,000 machine was available for $12,000, so I decided to take a risk and bring the engraving operations in-house. I hired a very detail-oriented lady named Maggy, who taught herself all about engraving. We put systems in place and started fulfilling orders. To my surprise, the error rate went down to almost zero, and more and more people came to us looking for rush custom orders. We began engraving many different styles of mugs and other products like mint julep cups and silver baby cups gifts. That side of the business continued to grow, and we had to buy a 2nd engraving machine!

During that first year of growing my business, I lived in a tiny room at a friend's house to get my rent and living expenses as low as possible. I had two part-time jobs to make sure I could pay the bills while I put all my savings and profit back into the business to pay for the inventory needed for the upcoming holiday season without taking on debt from outside funding.

This approach is a good thing to keep in mind when starting a business from scratch and at a place in life where this lifestyle is feasible. It's not uncommon for companies with excellent opportunities to fail because of under-capitalization, they just did not have enough money—staying power—to get solid enough footing for things to actually start rolling. Of course, there are other ways to fund your business like SBA (Small Business Administration) loans, angel investors or crowdfunding.

Here's another important piece of knowledge, and it might be one of the most valuable things I can personally share with you in this book: I wasn't a good importer when I started importing. I wasn't good at e-commerce when I built my first website. I took those first steps to make my business happen, despite not knowing everything and not being the 'best' at what I needed to do. Little by little I got better. I made some mistakes and learned from them as I went along. I worked in the business every day and didn't get discouraged by the many challenges that regularly came up.

> *"Don't be intimidated by what you don't know. That can be your greatest strength and ensure that you do things differently from everyone else."*
> —Sara Blakely, Spanx

Now I am good at both importing and e-commerce and have built the life I've always dreamed of, owning a successful business that gives me freedom to work anytime and anyplace. It has allowed me to spend more time with friends and family and work on relationships. And positive relationships and love are what I believe ultimately makes people happy.

After selling the business, I have more time to give back to my community and those around me. That is another way to bring more joy and happiness and create good karma in the world.

It's also given me the wherewithal to do something I had never dreamed of but realized—after hearing Marla Beck speak—I needed to do: to write a book, and include stories of other women entrepreneurs, and hope it makes a positive impact on many peoples' lives. I hope this book encourages other women to explore opportunities, to get out of their comfort zone, establish their independence, to travel somewhere on their own, and find a life where they are doing what makes them feel fulfilled and happy.

> *"I always did something I was a little not ready to do. I think that's how you grow. When there's that moment of 'Wow, I'm not really sure I can do this,' and you push through those moments, that's when you have a breakthrough."*
> —Marissa Mayer (CEO of Yahoo)

Perhaps you'll see some of your circumstances in my story, or in the stories that follow. Each of these entrepreneurs come from different backgrounds and different situations. Some of them faced and dealt with significant adversity or difficulties that spurred the need to start their own business.

After their stories, we'll continue with mine.

Necessity Can Pave the Way to Entrepreneurship

LORI AMES

"Be All You Can Be."
—U.S. ARMY

I sat in my son's hospital room in the Neurological Intensive Care Unit, wondering what the future would bring. All around him machines beeped, lights blinked, and the glow of numbers and data were displayed on screens and device displays. Rob was unresponsive. I was still too... unmoving in my chair in the corner, but my mind was racing. Few things—none that I can immediately think of—are harder than to be a parent and have something happen to your child. Especially when it's life-threatening, and there is nothing you can do but wait.

As time went on, thankfully Rob improved, and when he could talk, he asked, "Why aren't you at work?" He knew I always worked and me being there with him all day, for so many days, worried him.

"You're very sick," I told him. "I need to be with you."

"But, what about work, you need to be there, too, right?"

"Yes," I nodded, "but taking care of you is more important. I can't do that if I'm in the city (New York) every day."

"What about your job?"

After several years with a book publisher, I had joined a boutique public relations agency in New York City that specialized in book publicity. I had been with them 20 years when Rob, three weeks after his 22nd birthday was diagnosed with an inoperable malignant brain tumor. He knew that my career and work were important to me, and to us as a family. But the choice was clear, and I had made the decision while sitting with him at the hospital all those days. "I'm quitting my job to start my own business."

He looked at me questioningly. "But Mom..."

"It's the only way, Rob." At his worried look, I continued to explain, "I can't work in the city and see that you're cared for, that you get through all your chemo and radiation treatment appointments." I was the principal breadwinner for our family, which he knew and understood as well. "I can take all I've learned in nearly three decades in the publishing industry, and make a living for us," I said that boldly but honestly. With the length of time and difficulty of his recuperation, it was the only choice I had to make money and still be there for him. I'm not one to ask others for help so I couldn't fail. Sitting and plotting in the corner of his hospital room, I had worked out how to do it.

Born and raised on Long Island, New York where I still live (though further east than my parents who are still kicking at 86 and 89) I had learned a lot from my father and mother. Mom was a schoolteacher, Dad, an auto-mechanic. I was brought up with a strong work ethic and to appreciate what I had. I loved (love) my son and was going to work as hard as I possibly could to make my new business succeed.

And it—book publicity—is something I also love, which makes it easier to put in the effort required. I had role models, and mentors that inspired me throughout college and my career and what I'd learned from them would help me now. Back in school, wanting to enter the field of publishing, I had looked to Dick Marek, a publishing icon and one of my guest professors at Hofstra (I was an English major in a publishing studies track). He had a long, respected career. I also looked at women whom I respected. It sounds silly, but I admired Shirley Temple Black who went from child actress to having a successful political career and figured if she could do that, then anything was possible. And I learned a great deal about running a business and how to deal, and not deal, with clients from the agency I was with before my son became ill.

Starting a business to keep a semblance of normalcy when your child is traumatically ill borders on either brilliance or insanity. Some of the things you encounter can verge on both. One of the things I learned when I worked from home while Rob was still getting in-home therapy and nursing visits, is that cats can, and do, send emails (and one of mine even ordered groceries)! And that a dog will always wake up and bark when you are on a conference call with a client.

In the beginning, it was difficult balancing work responsibilities in between doctor visits and hospital stays. Some people believe that running your own business gives you the flexibility to have more vacations and free time. Ha! Not quite. In my situation, after I started my business, my son still had many treatments, some of which triggered more hospital visits. But with an iPad and laptop, I could stay connected and run my business whether we were in a doctor's office, chemo suite, or Pediatric Intensive Care Unit while he was sleeping.

A local weekly paper ran a story on us about a year after all this happened, to inspire others to see the light at the end of the tunnel and to offer hope in the face of adversity. I caught a little flack for starting a business while Rob was so sick. But sitting and just watching someone sleep doesn't make him or her better. Sitting there and being productive and creating a future does. When life handed me the unexpected, the challenge of having to choose either to focus on caring for my child or on my career, I picked my son. But I was also willing to take a risk to continue my career, using all my skills and experience gained over two-plus decades... by becoming self-employed, which gave me the means and flexibility to care for him.

About five months after I started the business, and when my son was done with the last of his major treatments, I realized working from home was no longer an option. I needed an animal free space and a place to store clients' books. I started thinking about finding a small office space close to home. My husband suggested looking on Craigslist, and I found an ad for office space that was available on the same road as we live. But there was no address listed to check it out. So, I printed the picture of the location's outside window and sent my husband walking up and down John Street to try and figure out where it was! Turns out, from our door to its door, was only 3/10ths of a mile. I met with the landlord, had a fellow small business owner come check it out, and signed a lease. That's also about when I realized it was time to bring on help. When a friend called to ask if I knew of a company that might have an internship available for his daughter, I hired her.

That decision, hiring my first employee and being responsible for the salary of another person, was the scariest part of starting my own business. Christina is still with me and is indispensable, but don't tell Rob, ha-ha, because he works here full-time now and is my other right hand!

Just as I've gone through significant changes over the last few years, so has my industry. We've both learned to evolve and adapt, but one thing is certain: books are still being published and always will be. The printed book has not died, despite the predictions of many. The biggest change is that now many more books are being self-published, and if done right, it's difficult to tell the difference between them and a trade book (conventionally or traditionally published). Whereas years ago, most of my clients were publishers, now many are authors.

What's changed the most is how we do publicity. It used to be you would mail out books, make phone calls, etc. Now it's about initiating outreach via email and arranging for much more guest content contributions, which aid in discoverability. Also, the traditional book publicity tour, city to city, is obsolete. With the advent of many types of technology, my business can handle projects and work with media around the world. We've also added building and managing social media platforms and web design for our clients, to our service offerings. All of which did not exist when I started in publishing.

Now I can Tweet and Facebook post with the best of them and share content to help my clients! I see growth, brilliance, and success ahead for my business. And that we are making an impact on an ever-changing industry.

I guess one of the biggest indicators that my business is viable and successful was when my Chase Small Business Banker came to me and offered me a line of credit. Woo Hoo, I felt I had made the big time!

* * *

Rob's illness has taught me that giving back is super important. We do pro bono work for both the Children's Brain Tumor Foundation and the Michael Magro Foundation because both organizations were extremely helpful to us and we want to make sure that we try to help others.

I've also learned so much about business that you don't learn when you're an employee. I feel if you're starting a business, you need to do—focus on—what you know. Use the skills and experience you've gained working for someone else and put them to work for your benefit.

Make the most of LinkedIn, or whichever social media platform is appropriate for what you do. And be nice to everyone. I can't stress this enough. Don't bad mouth anyone. The world is smaller than you think. Don't start your own business if you think it's going to give you more free time.

A new venture means you will—should—be working harder than you've ever worked before. Don't listen to the naysayers. Be organized. Find a banker, accountant, and lawyer who you can really, really count on. Most of all—and maybe this is the best piece of advice I can give you—you must believe in yourself!

Sometimes success is signing a new client; sometimes it's making time to leave the office and go to the gym. On other days, success may be making it through a round of bi-annual check-ups for my son. Life and business are fluid, so I like my definition of success to change as each situation arises.

About Lori Ames

Lori Ames has been involved in publishing and book publicity since the early 80s. After receiving her degree from Hofstra University in 1979, she worked briefly for a mass-market publisher and then began her career at a boutique book publicity agency in New York City. After more than three years there, she joined book publisher William Morrow where she remained for six years, advancing to the position of publicity director. During her tenure with William Morrow, she worked with many best-selling authors, celebrities, and sports figures. She returned to the boutique agency in 1991 where she remained until late 2010, helping run day-to-day operations, overseeing all publicity campaigns, and working on strategic planning to stay on top of new media while driving clients' books to the country's bestseller lists.

In late 2010, Lori's son was diagnosed with an inoperable malignant brain tumor, so she left the fast-paced world of Manhattan to care for her child and in the process set up her own business. Her son Robert is doing very well and plays a significant role in the company.

Lori serves on the Dean's Advisory Board of the Hofstra College of Liberal Arts and Sciences as well as on the Dean's Advisory Board for Hofstra University's Zarb School of Business Department of Marketing and International Business. She speaks regularly for the Introduction to Marketing classes at Hofstra's Zarb School of Business and has been a guest speaker at the National Speaker's Association's Mega Million Publishing Lab. She is sought after for her expertise, has written articles for outlets such as Speaker Magazine, and has been interviewed about her unintended entrepreneurial journey by the Long Island Press, Associated Press, and other outlets.

ThePRFreelancer, Inc.
WWW.THEPRFREELANCER.COM

ThePRFreelancer, Inc., is a public relations agency specializing in all aspects of publicity, public relations, and marketing for nonfiction book authors, particularly authors of business books.

Making Something Utilitarian Fashionable

STACEY BLUME

"To be nobody but yourself in a world which is doing its best, night and day, to make you everybody else—means to fight the hardest battle which any human being can fight; and never stop fighting."
—E. E. CUMMINGS

My journey away from what I thought was a safe plan for living a life that was truer to myself was neither easy nor traditional. Always a responsible person with an optimistic nature, I graduated from the University of Michigan and went on to UCLA, where I received my Masters in Social Work. The field of social work was a natural choice, as my family and friends often sought me out for my insightful and empathetic ear, and because I wanted to make a difference in this world. Although I was comfortably set on the path chosen, I soon felt pulled in a different direction, one filled with creativity and adventure.

In 2000, my father came to visit me in California where I was living and working at the time. While walking around shopping, we ended up in

Urban Outfitters where he noticed they carried the Dickies brand, an industrial-style clothing line. My father owns a commercial uniform company, and was especially surprised and amused that the utilitarian uniform look was considered 'fashion.' He turned to me and declared, "I've got a warehouse full of this stuff." That was the moment my entrepreneurial journey began and the seeds of what would soon become my own label, Blume, were planted.

With my father's comments dancing around in my head, I went back to New Jersey to visit his plant, saw the name tags, and imagined designs that were unlike anything else in the marketplace. Personalized patches on underwear! Whimsical, playful and relevant to the prevailing fashion trends, I was confident that combining the practical function of those industrial emblems with the sexiness of the thong would be a success.

Blume's personalized underwear was definitely unique, and there was an instantaneous response from my friends. They all wanted underwear embossed with their boyfriend or husband's name. Once again, family played an integral role in bringing this concept to fruition. My brother Brad, who managed the family uniform business, believed in me and the idea as well. He offered the infrastructure of the company and a financial investment of $30,000. With all the pieces in place, I had the working capital to buy inventory, build a website, participate in various trade shows, develop a myriad of marketing tools, and produce a photo shoot featuring my products. It was a labor of love and faith, one that fortunately had immediate positive results!

Blume officially launched in January 2003. Celebrities quickly caught on to this novel idea, and we made headlines when Jennifer Lopez celebrated her engagement to Ben Affleck by getting a 'Ben' name patch thong underwear. It was the height of the

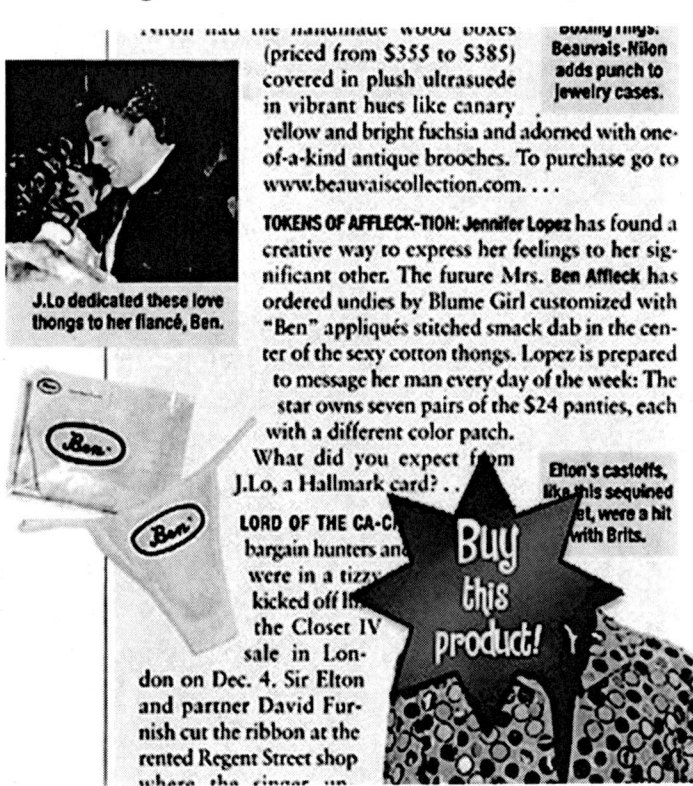

'Bennifer' phenomenon, so People Magazine and The Today Show reported that sexy scoop.

Boom! A trend was born, and Blume was on the map. The orders piled in faster than our seamstresses could sew. We made back the initial investment in the first three weeks, and suddenly the uniform factory became a house of style!

The success of the business was great, but the positive energy we created was just as fun. The factory was not used to being part of the glamorous world of fashion, and my father's and brother's employees loved it. It was great to see the guys in the warehouse singing Sisqo's *Thong Song,* which soon became prophetic when we found out through a store in London that Sisqo called to buy a Blume thong as a gift for his girlfriend! By the fall of 2005, I could set aside my social work career and focus on being a full-time entrepreneur.

Blume's organic growth put me through a boot camp type learning experience for the business of fashion. Our online website business was flourishing, and our first retail partners were high-end boutiques and department stores like Bloomingdales and Selfridges. We also designed a unique tower that held hundreds of thongs so that they could more easily sell in high-traffic tourist destinations like Las Vegas hotels. It created a fun impulse purchase by women who would spin the rack and find their guy's name.

Having a replenishment type of business model gave me the freedom to focus on other creative design extensions. The personalized underwear made great celebratory gifts for birthdays, anniversaries, Valentine's Day, and Christmas. Demand from bridal showers and bachelorette parties, both exciting occasions for custom items, also helped us expand the original concept. It didn't take long for the next innovative step to unfold. Many brides eventually become moms, and a baby's first uniform is a one-piece. It was a natural progression to move into baby clothing and a fun new market to tackle.

Blume made its mark on children's wear as it had with underwear, by again utilizing iconic name patches. The authentic emblems sewn on one-pieces, bibs, burp cloths, and tees became industrial—chic—customized favorites.

The children's business proved to be not only lucrative but creatively fulfilling as well. I decided to expand further on the designs, but this time, instead of only using patches, we went back to the warehouse and paired handmade ties made from bus driver's uniforms with tees and baby bodysuits. This simple, yet endearing style statement was soon to become another trendsetting success.

The infectious personality of these children's styles was snatched up by high-end retailers like Barneys and Saks, as well as by popular online shopping sites such as Diapers.com. Once again, Blume's unique designs caught the eye of entertainment's most famous celebrities. Blume's personalized and Little Man Tie Tees were spotted on the A-list tots of David and Victoria Beckham, Kourtney Kardashian, Tori Spelling, Mario Lopez as well as all four of Shaquille O'Neal's children. Just as it had before, the media picked up on what was trending in Hollywood and the progression of the Blume brand was again a success. We were featured in glossy magazines and digital media such as The Today Show, Good Morning America, Ellen, Rachael Ray, Access Hollywood, and Entertainment Tonight.

Although intended to be a comfortable and fun dress-up option for all children, the items retailed at Barney's for $56, which was a prohibitive amount for many families. Our success at the high-end of the retailing spectrum and the positive reaction we got from both our media features and celebrity fans led to interest from big-box retailers, like buy buy BABY, who wanted to offer these same designs for $14.99. While the interest from these type of mass retailers signaled our arrival as a major brand, it also presented our first real challenges.

Accommodating a lower price point would force us to rethink our manufacturing structure because all of Blume's items were produced domestically at the family's uniform union shop in New Jersey. I also resisted selling to the big-box retailers because even though Blume was a small business, we were profitable by selling less volume with higher margins. I was faced with a choice that many fast-growing companies must deal with at some point in their evolution.

Some of my entrepreneur friends encouraged me to give up the exclusivity of the high-end distribution and transition to selling to mass retailers. I wasn't convinced, but willing to explore the benefits of growing the business in that direction. Unlike before when I had the support of my family business to lean on, I needed to learn how to produce my product to reach a global size and scale.

I spent a year meeting a broad range of successful people in all areas of retail and fashion, as well as doing research on cut and sew manufacturers and dye houses. After extensively exploring alternative manufacturing options, I decided to partner with a company that had factories in China. They could finance the large production orders and had experience with the logistics support: packaging requirements, EDI, UPC codes, etc. They also had tech designers and product development employees that were dedicated to expanding Blume's offerings. I felt confident I had found an experienced team with which I could take the business to the next level.

The new manufacturing partner could deliver the large production orders while continuing to grow and expand our product lines to include outerwear, jeans, overalls, flannels, sleepers, blankets, socks, and other packaged accessories. We had come a long way from simple patches on a thong, and it was incredibly gratifying to watch all my design ideas come to life.

Design, development and managing the back-end of delivery were all valuable contributions to the manufacturing partnership. However, like many business relationships, not all our goals were aligned. The manufacturer did not want to cover any marketing expenses and did not see the benefit of selling to Blume's smaller specialty boutiques, the places that had helped put us on the map in the first place.

While I pushed to continue the relationship with the high-end stores and their clientele, they were adamant that their priority was about volume alone. My frustration with my new partners peaked the moment they told me: "We don't care about Blume, we only care about orders." I strongly believe that marketing and branding are the very things that lead to more sales. We were at an impasse, and I was ready to move on from this collaboration.

Although I had many leaders in the industry advising me along my way, I recognized the need for more formalized help and decided to establish an official Board of Advisors to help guide me on our next steps. This was a very positive development for Blume, as my board's invaluable experience and relationships were instrumental in securing a new partner who specialized in the baby market. We soon signed a licensing deal with a company who was willing to participate in tradeshows, agreed to produce exclusive designs for Blume's high-end customers, and paid me as a Creative Director.

With this new licensor in place, I felt supported in my overall vision and successfully expanded our distribution beyond Nordstrom, buy buy BABY, Babies R Us, with more retailers including Dillard's, TJ MAX, and Burlington.

We were on our way, but unfortunately, my new partner ultimately did not care about the integrity and growth of the Blume brand or the trust I thought we had established. It was a setback, and I was discouraged, but quickly recognized where I made mistakes and worked to correct them.

Despite my success in building the Blume brand, I was still a novice in licensing partnerships, and some things hadn't occurred to me while negotiating my legal agreement with the new licensor. In particular, the licensor changed factories during our second year, and this new facility did not maintain the higher-end quality of Blume's goods. The items that were shipped later into our arrangement were made by their preferred suppliers who most likely gave them cheaper costs resulting in bigger profit margins. I didn't realize they would want to change facilities and had nothing in writing that allowed me to influence the decision. Other issues soon began to emerge.

My new partner limited product development and did little sampling of new designs. It wasn't until later that I realized this was part of their 'bait and switch' tactics. The problems began to mount. I was informed that some of the reorders from current retailers did not meet their minimum order quantities (also known as MOQs). Rather than try to involve me in finding a solution to this problem, they simply canceled the entire order. Even worse, despite their refusal to produce and deliver Blume's collections, I discovered that the licensing partner went around me and substituted those reorders with their in-house brand (that they did not have to pay a royalty on) rather than the original requested Blume merchandise.

Combined, these issues proved to be a hard-earned lesson learned regarding the importance of having a binding licensing agreement that protects the brand's quality and existing retail relationships as well as requirements connected to product development and sampling. While costly, the lessons ensured that I would never enter another licensing deal without defined minimum guaranteed royalties (known as MGRs). Having the MGR would have helped align our expectations and motivated the licensing partner to keep Blume stocked on the shelves instead of letting the brand slowly cycle out.

The transitions from controlling all aspects of the business (manufacturing, marketing, distribution) to contracting it to vendors (yet remaining involved in the process) to purely hands-off licensing, personified that 'battle' E.E. Cummings referred to at the beginning of this chapter. That experience convinced me to always stay true to myself. Rather than give up maintained the optimism that has always served me so well and decided that the natural step for me and my brand was to move ahead with other innovative designs in different apparel categories that I had been working on behind the scenes for years.

When the owner of a chic Los Angeles retail shop, who was already selling Blume's women's thongs in huge amounts, called to order men's underwear with ladies' names. I had to explain that of course, that was a part of the vision, but they didn't exist yet. I noticed that most men's underwear companies labeled their brand name across the waistband. A man's torso is a sexy piece of real estate and muddying that with a brand's name struck me as a very odd common practice.

I had the idea to showcase the man's torso with a sweatband attached as a waistband! The color stripes would provide a new aesthetic of fashion flair, while the soft terry loops would be extremely comfortable with sweat absorbing functionality.

I realized that using a sweatband as elastic could be applied to other silhouettes, and would also work perfectly for women when utilized on a sports bra, yoga pants, and as bag handles that help absorbs weight and sits more comfortably on shoulders.

The excitement of these unique product ideas overwhelmed me, and that familiar feeling took over. I felt compelled to act on this new mission. I had been knocked off by other brands with the name patch thongs and the baby collections, so knew my next idea needed to be legally protected.

I was more prepared now, and aware of all the hard work and capital involved to successfully produce, market and distribute apparel. This time, I realized that obtaining patents on the idea and then licensing to global brands could be a smart and lucrative route. I wanted to do this with the utmost care and spent a year researching patent attorneys before hiring a top firm to successfully obtain eight patents for underwear, loungewear, activewear and accessory bags.

Once my patents were published, I contacted

a global athletic brand and pitched them my idea. The executive said, "I believe innovation drives the market and if you have something new, then I want to see it."

I was elated and flew to California to meet with them two weeks later, armed with a video presentation and my rough samples in hand. They embraced the concept right away and were as excited as I was by the purity and simplicity of these never before seen products.

They set a follow-up meeting with the heads of business and product development at their US headquarters who were also impressed and asked, "Are you telling me that this idea is so simple and no one here thought of it?"

We went back and forth for a few weeks exploring the opportunity, and it was explained that their company worked four years out for product planning and that everything needed to be approved by their European headquarters. The company also preferred a 'proof of concept' before committing to new initiatives. However, they were happy to stay in touch and provide feedback to continue helping to get the idea market ready.

Testing the market required an actual working prototype, more than my current rough samples, so I switched gears to create the product under the Blume brand, rather than selling the concept by licensing the patents. I met with one of the largest elastic manufacturers in the world, a company new to me but not to the world of apparel.

This was the start of another long process of product development as their technical teams had to work with new machines and yarns to develop a working sweatband that could be attached to apparel as elastic. We went through many different versions of densities, modulus, tension, elasticity, proper elongation, and shrinkage. I had no way of knowing that turning an ordinary sweatband into a functioning piece of elastic would be so difficult! Even though this was another labor of love, it has proved to be a much more challenging goal to achieve. However, my experiences make me confident in my ability to manifest the vision that will be Blume Sweats.

As a self-funded entrepreneur, I have made my share of mistakes and earned an invaluable education while realizing my dreams. It is now time for me to reach further and engage the support of the right investors. I am confident in this new approach because I already received great feedback on the patented designs from global brands. My new financial model includes revenue from licensing, a solution that not only lowers risks but offers potentially higher returns.

I haven't stopped trying to learn either, and seek out resources to help me become better informed on potential deal structures.

The fundraising process has its own set of

challenges, but I feel incredibly empowered by the new knowledge and experience I'm getting from it.

Evolving Blume into a more sophisticated corporate structure with investors required an understanding of things like a Board of Directors, advisory agreements, stock option agreements, and convertible notes. But the learning process has kept me energized and committed to making it happen.

The patented collections are a differentiated product in a crowded market. They are also legally protected and defensible. The plan is to launch these innovative designs and scale in multiple categories so that everyone can experience the comfort, fashion, and function of sweatband elastic!

I've learned that if you are passionate about your vision, just keep taking steps to move your project forward. Get organized, absorb as much information as you can, stay positive and have faith that the right people and circumstances will come together. Think of obstacles as opportunities to grow and remember building a business is a 'battle' worth winning.

After a long and challenging journey, I've come to realize that success—to me—is having the freedom to pursue and achieve my dreams. That's what inspires me and makes me so passionate about my creative ideas. That's how I've built my business.

About Stacey Blume

Before launching her business, Stacey graduated from the University of Michigan with a Bachelor of Arts (B.A.) in Psychology, went on to earn a Masters of Social Work at UCLA and worked with a variety of children's causes.

Concurrent with establishing her original clothing lines, Stacey has been working on bringing her 'next big idea' to fruition: patented underwear, activewear, loungewear and accessory collections that are set to launch in 2017. Stacey's passion and drive have kept her energized on an exciting entrepreneurial journey.

Blume
WWW.BLUMEGIRL.COM

Blume launched in 2003 with a unique and sexy way for women to surprise that special someone. Personalized underwear is a perfect fun gift for every occasion- some couples get tattoos to symbolize their love, but these custom intimates are a lot more fun and much less painful! Classic, boring monogramming got a chic new makeover with Blume's iconic workman's patch—any name can be inscribed on the industrial emblem. Personalized fashions are available for the whole family to enjoy, including dogs! Blume's unique sense of style and playful sensibility have been distributed in high-end stores as well as big-box retailers around the country and internationally.

It's Your Life... Own It

JENNY DORSEY

"It's your life. Make your choices and own up to it."

-JENNY DORSEY

One of the greatest challenges in my career and life has been my relationship with my family. My parents instilled in me—at a young age—a sense of inferiority and never being good enough. Early on I developed a reluctance to accept compliments or acknowledge my own abilities and became good at blaming myself for things beyond my control.

This mental paradigm haunted me for years. Breaking an expensive glass by accident would cost me a week's worth of sleep thinking about why I had positioned my elbow the wrong way. I grew up haggard with self-hate that resulted in prolonged bouts of depression and suicide attempts.

For years, I shrugged off therapy because, 'I didn't need it,' but really, it was because I didn't believe I deserved it or that there was a better life out there for me.

After struggling with a lifetime of depression, anxiety, confusion, and insecurity, I finally realized I needed to do what I wanted. Living based on what my family expected had caused me so much pain. I couldn't go on like that. Once I began making decisions for myself, especially when I chose to go to culinary school, my family and I barely talked. Within the last few months, we have cut off ties completely.

It all came to a head at my wedding last year: my mother recounted her impressions of my youth to present day: She stood in front of my, and my husband Matt's, wedding guests to declaim, "I remember when Jenny was five. That was my favorite time. She was so happy; she was always curious about everything. But as she grew older she became different, I felt I was losing the string of my kite. And now, she's a changed young woman. I'm so glad she found Matt. Maybe I still don't understand her decisions, but Matt does, and he's there to be with her."

While I know, she meant what she said as extending an olive branch, to me it felt like a subtle reminder that in her eyes, I was still not good enough—not able to make the right decisions for myself. It's been devastating to see how little she and my father can budge from their preconceived notions, but I have slowly used that as fuel to grow stronger mentally as I continue to learn, mature, and become the woman I want to be.

That strengthening and toughening has kept me going through the challenges of starting and running a business, especially in the hypercompetitive, saturated food and beverage industry.

I came from a Chinese immigrant family and moved to the United States when I was three years old. My parents are traditionalists, overbearing and narrow in their definition of success. I'm an only child, so my upbringing was a manifestation of all the desires and wishes they had to leave behind upon immigrating here.

My mother wanted a sweet, submissive, soft-spoken, family-oriented daughter; my father wanted an ambitious, smart, successful, financially stable career woman. As I grew up, I grappled with their conflicting desires which were, in many ways, diametrically the opposite of my personality: I'm free spirited, very opinionated, inherently thoughtful and defiant of social norms. Because I did not fit either mold they had planned for me, my early adulthood was a series of bizarre compromises: I started college at 15 (ambitious) but went to a state school and lived at home for two years (submissive, family-oriented). I switched from marketing to a finance degree (seen as more successful), but instead of becoming an investment banker I chose to be a management consultant (troubling to my father because the pay was significantly less).

In 2010, I graduated with a B.A. in Finance from the University of Washington and rebelliously decided to start my first job in NYC, in management consulting within the fashion and luxury goods industry, but visited home in Seattle every three months. I found my work to be unfulfilling and superficial but was addicted to the 'glamorous' lifestyle, the clothes, parties, and money. Eventually, I burnt out, so I decided to apply early to Columbia Business School's Class of 2014 and escape the grind for a few years. I was accepted as their youngest-ever admit at 21 but was still chastised by my parents for not instead applying to Harvard. When I was admitted in December of 2011, I had a solid eight months before starting the MBA program full-time and made an off-kilter decision that changed everything.

I have always loved to cook—and I definitely love to eat—so it's not surprising I gravitated toward something food-related. While waiting to start my MBA, I decided to 'try out' the culinary world. But I'm not someone to do anything halfway, so instead of taking some intensive recreational classes, I had to go for an official Diploma in Culinary Arts at the Institute of Culinary Education (NYC). I didn't think the change would be permanent; I still remember strolling into the admissions office and paying half of the tuition with my credit card (clearly, I hadn't learned much in my Finance classes). It may have been done on a whim, but by the time I graduated from that program, I realized I wanted to work in food full-time. My friends thought I was crazy. But I couldn't bear the thought of another year in management consulting, even if it was a more logical career path with a potential to make more money. So, in January 2013, I decided to leave Columbia and pursue the world of food full-time.

At first, I had a tough time finding a job that utilized both my culinary and business skill set. I did not seem to fit in anywhere and had to start from scratch. I willed myself to stop focusing on the title and pay but rather on what real skills could be learned from the position. If I could learn something useful from the work, I was willing to take the entry-level job. I was a barista, a fancy juice salesperson, a social media intern, a PR assistant, and (of course) a kitchen cook, among other oddities.

Eventually, I found a 'dream job' as the Global Food & Beverage Associate at Le Pain Quotidien (LPQ). I was involved with the entire menu development process, from research and development (R&D) to launch, across multiple countries. I loved my work and realized there was a role out there for me that could combine what I wanted to do in the kitchen (experiment, test, learn, play) with my critical thinking abilities and business savvy.

After I had left LPQ, I began to build a book of business for myself focusing on menu R&D mixed with the business strategy skills I had from management consulting. My first client (whom I continued to work with for years) was a nutritionist needing a chef to put together a comprehensive meal plan and recipes for a vegan, diabetic-friendly cookbook. I'd done some work with vegan food at LPQ but little in the diabetic area, so I was excited by the opportunity to extend my R&D scope. I remember being incredibly nervous, always suffering from imposter syndrome—worried she wouldn't like my recipes or would feel I was too expensive.

As months passed, it was apparent how satisfied she was with my work. That gave me the confidence I could do any job if I worked hard and felt passionate about it. Freelancing is something I had never done before, but after my first gig, I began pursuing more opportunities, big and small. Many times, I took on work I hadn't ever done before. I knew I couldn't sell myself to clients on years and years of experience, but I could on pure drive and determination.

After three years of freelancing with many food businesses, I had built my roster of clients from a few small businesses to global chains, upscale restaurants, food media, food products, hardwares, and a variety of startups (food and non). I decided to officially incorporate my LLC in January 2016. It's been an incredible ride, and I absolutely love being able to play a foundational and meaningful part in a food business's life cycle: intelligently helping navigate a complicated industry and build a strong platform for my clients. I'm proud of how I've grown into a role beyond developing menus to become a trusted advisor and thought leader in the space.

Leaving my Columbia MBA program to pursue the unknown path of a food career has been, and probably will always be, a pivotal moment of my life. To many who knew me and for a while, even to myself, it felt like a decision that had happened overnight. But now in hindsight, I can see it was born over decades spent letting everyone else dictate how I lived my life. While some of them had good intentions, their opinions were irrelevant because it was not what I wanted. Those three freelancing years were a struggle, but as I worked through them, I learned that if I held true to myself, something would come. That was not the approach I had taken with everything in my life up until then, and sometimes I laugh at how much I tormented my younger self because I had prioritized wanting to fit in instead of growing into my own person. I still remember in my early 20s, I wanted to be a stylish, cute, fun girly-girl that everyone liked. It was a front, I was a fake, and I would always end up dating these awful, misogynist guys. When I dropped the façade and became my opinionated, tee-shirt wearing, no makeup, sometimes cursing, self I met my soulmate (and now husband). He loves me for who I am, is excited by my intensity and passion, and has supported me through some of the most challenging stages of my career while growing my business.

My opinionated self always finds a way to make every concept my 'own.' My husband and I also have a passion project, a supper club named, Wednesdays. We started it after meeting at Columbia to gather together the peers we enjoyed at school but had difficulty bridging into personal connections, in a comfortable environment where we could engage on a deeper level. Naturally, I wanted to cook and my husband, a self-taught mixologist, wanted to make drinks.

One thing led to another, and we began to host these underground tasting dinners on a regular basis. Strangers started coming, intrigued by our concept and wanting a different experience from that of going to a regular restaurant.

In the beginning, I desperately wanted my dinners to be the cool, fancy dinner series that took over NYC because I was still looking for self-validation. After the initial high of simply having new people at the table, we realized we needed more press, media traction, and consistency to regularly fill our seats. But I soon discovered that our approach wasn't working. So we took a good, hard look at ourselves and realized we'd been 'barking up the wrong tree,' targeting our brand at snobby people who didn't care about our greater mission while serving food to 'please the masses' and wouldn't inspire anyone to return.

Once I dropped the pretense and served the bold food I wanted and told diners to show up with real personalities instead of beautiful clothes, our tickets began to sell out within the hour. Again and again, I've realized there is a *right thing* for everyone in life, you just have to keep working and exploring until you find it. Mine is to drop the pretense and display who I am— that's what I've always craved to be able to do. I've known it was the right path all along, all I need to do is to not be too afraid to follow it.

I still remember the first private event I hosted for Wednesdays happened to fall on a day when my husband was out of town. Out of pure hubris, I figured I would cajole two of my friends to help, and I would run the show. No problem! This was back when our dog, an 8-year-old pit bull mix named King Arthur, was still allowed to roam around in the kitchen as I cooked for guests. If this already sounds like a recipe for disaster, rest assured it was!

The event got off to an okay start; the dinner was for a woman who had just been promoted, so the champagne and celebratory vibe kept the enthusiasm high as the night began. However, it quickly took a nosedive. As I scrambled around the kitchen, completely 'in the weeds' (culinary speak for being severely behind schedule), my friend-helpers wandered around the room, under-utilized and confused. Neither of them knew the order of the dishes (I forgot to brief them on the food), or how the dinner usually operated (they'd never attended one) and where everything was located in the place.

Beef Tartare, Photo Credit Sara Snyder

I thought we had turned the corner when we approached the main entrée: Beef Wellington. 'Whew,' I thought, 'just this and dessert and we're done!' I was so busy daydreaming about finishing up service, I managed to drop the entirety of the Wellington as I transferred it from the oven to the cutting board. A quarter of the carefully crafted filet mignon was promptly gobbled up by King Arthur. My two friends panicked. I panicked and burst into tears. We stared at each other and began arguing in hushed voices about what we should do. During this, I could hear the semi-inebriated women starting to get impatient out in the event room. Luckily, I remembered I had some extra beef in the fridge, and while it was not wrapped in puff pastry and smothered in my signature shiitake-Chinese sausage mix, it was enough to pair with the small slice of Wellington I divvied out to each person.

As the three of us marched out with plates in hand, I put on a smile and kept telling myself, 'fake it till you make it.' Amazingly, our guests had no idea and even cheered at how tasty their entrée was! I learned so many lessons in that horrifying 15 seconds between dropping the meat and it going down King Arthur's gullet. But primarily this: perception is not always reality, so sometimes you are the only person who knows things did not go as planned. Ever since then, however, I've never underestimated the importance of being over-prepared and communicating extensively for all events and having a secure team in place!

To date, we've held over 100 dinners, served 1,000+ people with our largest pop-up restaurant being attended by 100 guests in the beautiful Old Bowery Station in NYC.

* * *

I've come a long way in just a few short years, and it struck me recently how far they have taken me. My husband, knowing how I had struggled with self-doubt for years, sat me down and showed me the press page on my website.

"There," he told me as he clicked at the top and began scrolling through reviews, interviews, and articles about me and our business. "You did all of that." He paused at one item on the site page, my appearance on *Cutthroat Kitchen*, the first of my four appearances on The Food Network so far.

I began to sputter and make excuses. "You know my friend from culinary school referred me to that show, so it's not like I did anything."

"Really," he said. "Did she force the producers to recommend you to *Beat Bobby Flay* too?"

"Well, they only wanted me on the show because they needed a token Asian person," I argued.

"Oh, really," he said, "and they also forced you to win?"

"Okay whatever," I said. "And you know those Oxygen Network people (another TV feature I was part of) just wanted a 'food' thing."

"Mmhmm," he responded. "There are a million 'food' things in New York City, but it just so happens you got it by pure chance? Who made you apply and interview?"

This continued for a good hour before I finally conceded, "Fine, maybe I did some of those things, and they are cool."

He grinned at me, "Okay—we're making progress—now repeat that statement a few times with more confidence."

I did so awkwardly before muttering darkly and throwing up my hands in protest. This has happened before, but for some reason, I truly listened to him this time. I did deserve better because I had hustled and worked hard to get to where I am today. I deserve the cheers and congratulations. But most importantly, I deserve to be happy and proud inside. We then sat down, analyzed our finances, and set aside a budget for me to go to therapy every week. Therapy has truly changed my life, from my outlook for the future to the kindness I use to view myself and accept from others. It also prompted me to open up publicly about my depression in hopes I could inspire others to also realize they deserve to be happy and to pursue help if they need it. Since doing so, I've already had more than a half-dozen people email, message, or tell me in person how much it meant to them that someone they 'admired' (me?!) admitted having such damning thoughts about themselves. It's made me realize I've been given this place in the world so I can make a difference, and it is as simple as telling everyone the truth.

Where I'm at now, both professionally and personally, is something I'm tremendously grateful for and appreciative of. My consulting business continues to grow dramatically, mostly organically or through referrals. Wednesdays has been featured in almost all the notable food media outlets critical to the NYC or SF food scene, most recently making a Top-10 list on Business Insider and Thrillist. Now, I'm focusing my attention on starting a new business with two other founders named '10X.' It's a co-working space specifically geared toward food, beverage and hospitality entrepreneurs, professionals, and small businesses. My goal is to grow it into a venture-backed company with a culture that emphasizes work and life balance and caters to different types of personalities: no set hours, no politics, no bullshit, strong incentives matched to what each employee wants and is motivated by.

Our society is entrenched in a depressing way to work, and I believe it will take a mountain (of women) to change that. My endgame and destination are to make an impact on how we live and work. All long, important, journeys start with just one step, and my ultimate goal is to be a career coach and motivational speaker. I've recently started a career counseling arm of my consulting business and have already begun working with a few women who are transitioning into the food world after years in a thankless corporate career. It is one of the most rewarding things I've ever done to date.

I was very moved by the book *Quiet* by Susan Cain, and it has motivated me to think more deeply about how I can help people learn to accept themselves. I'm an extroverted introvert and have many times found myself confused and lost in a society so strongly geared toward extroverted demonstrations of leadership and confidence. As a female entrepreneur, I've also found myself conflicted in how I should act and grow as a businesswoman to fulfill the male-dominated stereotypes of success and authority. There exists a slew of articles such as *5 Tricks to Make Your Emails More Authoritative as a Female* or *How to Discuss X with Male Coworkers*. But we do not need to be told how to act; those are not molds we need to fit into.

As women, we don't need to be more like men to be successful. Just as Cain has made it a mission to inspire people through exploring and celebrating the achievements of introverts, I hope to do the same by showing others they need not listen to others as to what is 'right' and 'best' but instead follow their own journey of self-discovery. Here are my personal beliefs, that have helped me go from 'doubt to doing':

- There is never a convenient time to take the leap.
- If you do not believe in yourself, you cannot succeed. Bravado does not count.

- If there is something that is negatively impacting your life, cut it out. No matter how hard, no matter how 'wrong,' it is your life, and you must come first. No one else will put you first.
- Find your real friends. They are ones you do not hesitate to fail in front of.
- Your time is the most valuable thing you have, stop wasting it on people or ideas and thoughts that do not deserve it.
- You deserve your accomplishments. You deserve your accolades. You deserve everything you have.
- The only person who can say 'no' to you is yourself.
- There is no single right way to live for everyone. There is only the way you discover that is right for you.
- You already know what you want. You are the only person in your way to getting it.
- If you do not have a bigger picture, larger mission, some sort of giving desire for your life you will indeed find life is meaningless.
- Seriously, do what YOU f*cking want to do!

Success to me means waking up every day and never feeling like I'm 'working' because what I do is my passion and serves a bigger purpose than my own needs. Believing that my work, in some small way, makes an impact and contributes to the change I want to see in the world. Success is also freeing: not worrying about titles like Forbes 30 Under 30 or being hung up on the opinions of others. Finally, success is being able to speak freely and confide in the people I surround myself with, the people I care about the most and the people who love and accept my authentic self.

ABOUT JENNY DORSEY

Jenny Dorsey, Photo Credit Nanette Wong

Jenny is an entrepreneur, professional chef, business and culinary consultant, based in New York City.

She is also the Co-Founder and Executive Chef of the popular supper club, Wednesdays. Jenny holds a B.A. in Finance from the University of Washington, a Diploma in Culinary Arts from the Institute of Culinary Education and was an MBA Candidate at Columbia Business School. Jenny started her career as a management consultant at Accenture, working with fashion & luxury brands on strategic planning and operations. Since moving into the food realm, she has led menu development for Le Pain Quotidien in three countries in addition to working at various fine-dining restaurants across the country, most recently 2-

Michelin-starred Atera in New York City. Jenny has also been awarded culinary grants from both the Bocuse d'Or and James Beard Foundations to further her practice.

Jenny Dorsey Culinary Consulting
WWW.JENNYDORSEYCONSULTING.COM

Jenny Dorsey Culinary Consulting specializes in menu R&D and business strategy for all types of food companies. Wednesdays is an underground dinner tasting restaurant—or 'supper club'—based in New York City. Its concept is simple: make the dinner conversation as enjoyable as the meal itself. Meals consist of seven courses paired with a 4-course cocktail flight. Large format pop-up dinners are hosted in various venues around the city and small bi-monthly dinners at the 'head-eatery,' a brick-lined loft in Chelsea. Guests are seated around a wooden communal table and the evening progresses with a series of interesting, semi-bizarre prompts to help guests connect and engage on the deeper level while enjoying Michelin-caliber food & drink in a relaxed, comfortable, inviting environment.

Creating the Brand That Changed an Industry

CARRIE HAMMER

"Most women are dissatisfied with their appearance, it's the stuff that fuels the beauty and fashion industries."
—ANNIE LENNOX

The reasons for starting a business can evolve over time, which can then change a business plan into the owner's real mission.

That's what I experienced, and I'm sure many other entrepreneurs have encountered something similar. I discovered the first inkling of my company's purpose in New Jersey at a hair show whose models my fashion line had been selected to dress. When I arrived, the first model for the show was being worked on, hair and makeup. As I waited for her to finish, I was astonished at how young she looked. I could not believe she was in the show. "How old are you?"

"Twelve," she said.

I was even more stunned by that statement. Not long after they were finished with her, I—with all kinds of reservations running through my mind—dressed and styled her. When done, she looked like she was 30 years old.

Another moment and event that shaped my business—and its mission—was New York Fashion Week in 2014. I was launching my namesake line and viewed the models for the show, but I could not envision them wearing my clothes down the runway. My clients were diverse: executives, CEOs, doctors, activists... a variety of extraordinary women—different shapes and sizes. Not mass-produced and packaged, their beauty was unique. I contacted my clients and recruited them to walk the runway wearing my clothes. And as they did, it showed that this is what beauty looks like when it's not artificially sculpted—produced—for mere surface appearance. They were much more than the objectified women so often presented in magazines and shows. They were (are) Role Models Not Runway Models™. And that phrase now defines what I want to accomplish in the Beauty & Fashion industry: a reshaping of attitude and perception of what beauty truly is, and that it comes in all forms and sizes.

At that New York event, we also made history when one of my clients, a doctor, who had never been defined by her disability, rolled the runway and rocked the attendees and media. We (she and I) received many emails from women and girls around the world who, when they saw or heard about it, felt for the first time that their disability did not limit them being beautiful, too. That their disability did not define them any more than my blue eyes defined me.

What happened at that event has helped begin breaking down barriers and eliminating stereotypes in the industry. I'm just one designer, but we've started a movement that now counts over 30 brands that now include diversity in their models on the runway and in their advertising and marketing. This collective effort will create a huge groundswell of support to change, globally, how we define beauty. It will reveal what consumers actually want to see, wear and be. My company will be part of that evolution.

But I started with a personal need...

* * *

Working in advertising, a young executive doing really well, on a team with mostly older other executives, I felt I needed to excel at dressing as an executive. That sartorial sharpness could be distinctive, but I was frustrated with trying to find clothing for work. Nothing felt like me. There was a huge gap between the quality, look and feel of affordable clothing for professional women and the fashionable high-end, which I couldn't afford.

I've always loved fashion—the feeling of well-made and elegantly styled clothing—so dressing well was paramount to me. As a part of my job, I routinely met with Chief Marketing Officers from companies, like HBO and The Discovery Channel. Again, what I wore could be a distinguishing personal brand. I knew what I wanted and what would suit me but just couldn't find it.

Necessity, as they say, is the mother of invention. I started creating the kind of clothing I was looking for. I spoke with tailors and had them turn my designs into clothing just for me.

People would stop me on the street and tell me, "Oh my God... I love that dress! I love that jacket!" And that's when I realized, wow it's not just me, other people are looking for alternatives as well. It was one of those moments when things fell into place. Though I had no experience in the fashion industry, I came from a family of artists and their artistic sensibility carried onto me.

I was raised by two entrepreneur parents, and they served as incredible role models for me. When you see your parents taking business risks and showing that you can establish your own rules and that sometimes you can even break old-fashioned long-held conventional rules... it dramatically impacts your understanding of how business is done. And that it's not just following the status quo. That certainly shaped my vision of how my business could be created.

My mother had her own graphic design and advertising agency, and on her side of the family, I came from a line of famous artists. I was very, very lucky to have two parents who brought home lessons about business every day and to see how artists create things from nothing but ideas and concepts... even how they live their lives.

Now, I didn't realize that at the time but now as an adult, I can see how very rare that is for a child.

I remember growing up that everything—in a good way—was a negotiation. Anytime I wanted something, my parents would tell me, "Draw up a contract or an offer, and we'll discuss it." They would make me do a presentation, and then a decision would be made. I also learned about budgets. Specifically, my allowance, which was performance-based... there was a chart on the fridge of things I had to do. When I accomplished them—did my work—I got a star, and the number of stars earned dictated how large my allowance was. At an early age, I came to understand fully how work, job performance, and your income are interrelated. That taught me a valuable lesson, as well.

My parents always encouraged me to pursue my passions. And it wasn't so much a particular conversation about the topic or interest, but more that they showed it through their own actions. When they were passionately engaged in some business project, I watched them, and they became very easy personal models to follow. They led—perhaps without meaning to—by example. When I would express interest in something, they would tell me, "That's great let's explore it and plan to find out more." So, there was always the thought—my idea or interest—then discussion to look at all sides and then it was followed by action. Results were tied to both thought and action, and that is a great lesson for a young person, too.

My parents would give me the support and encouragement, but it was up to me to make it happen. And the inference was that if I wanted it bad enough, I would do what I needed to do to accomplish it.

When I came to the realization that other female business executives needed clothing alternatives, and it could be a business opportunity, I had a foundation that grounded me. But still, the scariest part of starting and running a business was literally just taking the first step, getting started. What I was thinking of doing was a huge departure from my career path and 180° in a different direction. Going from being an advertising executive and entering the fashion industry, which I had virtually no experience in, was a monumental decision. Yet, I felt compelled to make the leap.

And then I had to tell my family friends and colleagues about my decision. Which of course created all kinds of questions I had to answer and reinforced the magnitude of the pronouncement. That made it even more terrifying. Not just their questions, but the questions I began to ask myself. I had convinced myself that I was willing to step up, to take the risk, but inside wrestled with the thought of having to tell people if I failed. I had told everyone about my plans, so I wasn't flying under the radar. I had to reconcile the fact that if I were unsuccessful, it would be public. That was the hardest part for me... thinking all those things and then still moving forward to start the business.

Ever since then, to make sure that I don't fail, I've had to figure it out. You don't know what you don't know as an entrepreneur. You work your way through learning and then executing—doing—what you've just learned.

One of those first things I worked out was how to use Kickstarter (a venue to help find resources and support to help make your idea a reality). I was one of their first fashion campaigns when Kickstarter was relatively new. When I researched it, I realized what an innovative way of fundraising it could be. Not only did it turn into a way of raising some funds for my startup, but it also created new customers, pre-orders and media exposure for me. I marketed and promoted my campaign through my personal contacts and social media, which got enough people initially interested for it to gain momentum and spread virally.

As I got my business rolling, I never considered trying to get my clothing into retailers, which meant offering it at wholesale to stores. All our sales, from the beginning, were online and direct to my customers, most of which are CEOs and executives who don't have time to shop in stores. The exclusive nature of our relationship ensures price support and a measure of loyalty. That means though we are always acquiring new clients, we don't have to continually 're-sell' our customer base. Understanding who your clientele or customers are is critical to building a sustainable business.

Another excellent piece of advice for all entrepreneurs is to not reinvent the wheel. An example, for me, is that we use a third-party warehouse. Warehousing and fulfillment are not a business I want to be in so we use vendors to provide services that are not part of our core business. As much as I love Manhattan's Garment District, I also did not want to become a manufacturer. We just could not get our cost of goods and pricing in line domestically, so we contract our manufacturing to overseas companies. But it was important that I visit with these manufacturing partners to see their operations and understand how they conducted their business. Doing that made me more comfortable with my decision to utilize them. I did learn through making some bad choices early on and placing orders with manufacturers that did not work out as reliable partners.

And I think that's something that all product-based companies go through when starting out. It's kind of like dating, you have to kiss a few frogs before you find the right one.

There are so many things I've learned that it would be impossible to talk about them all here, but this is probably the single most important: you must be willing to make decisions that can lead to mistakes. That's the only way that you learn about business—your business—and there's no option or alternative. This goes back to that fear you have when starting out. You must push forward and just act if the business you want to start is crucial to you. You can't be afraid of making the wrong call, the bad decision. You make it, and then you deal with the outcome. Each and every time. That's how you learn what works and what doesn't. And this is an important qualifier, you need to see what works best and that feels right for both you as an individual and as a business.

Here's an example: when I started my business, I wanted to focus on nothing but custom work. Which means one product at a time, designed specifically for one customer. Well, that's not scalable, and there's no way that pricing in my market would make that a sustainable business model. I course corrected to doing ready-to-wear products, and that's proven to be better for me, my business and my customers. It gives them both a unique product more in line with what they want and at an affordable price point.

You must be agile in business, especially if you're in a very competitive industry. That agility can help you carve out—and defend—your niche. In the beginning, I wasn't very flexible but I've learned, and now I am extraordinarily so.

I've learned to listen to my customers, and that tells me what—and who—my market is. And that's probably the most important thing to do especially early on; keep your ear to the ground and listen to what your customers and clients say. Then adapt accordingly.

When I'm designing new lines and new products, I'm in touch with my existing customers directly so I can get their feedback. That helps me adjust what I'm working on, and to hone in on where I should focus. I'll ask my clients, what are you missing in your wardrobe? What do you wish you had? What do you see that you love, or what do you dislike? What do you have in your wardrobe that you wish you could replicate? These are the types of questions that any entrepreneur could modify for their product or service to ask their clients to get more insight to better position their company in their market.

So, I've circled back to what I touched on in the opening of this chapter. The process of defining and refining that determines who and what you are and what you become. That evolution—when realized—can empower you to reach people, and though your company may not provide or produce a product used at the individual or consumer level, your market is still made up of people. And those people will always respond best to authenticity. That's what drives my company to success, and perhaps it might work well for you, too.

> *"Beauty is not caused. It is."*
> —Emily Dickinson

Success is following my 'true north' vs. 'magnetic north' — following my virtues, values, and beliefs rather than what others want or what society expects of me. As long as I'm making decisions that follow my values, I consider that success.

ABOUT CARRIE HAMMER

Carrie Hammer started her career as an advertising sales executive and often heard that she should 'dress for the job she wanted not the job she had,' so she created her eponymous clothing line CARRIE HAMMER in 2012 to deliver stylish professional wear to women. Hammer has been credited in kick-starting the 'body positive' movement in the fashion and advertising industries through the creation of her powerful campaign: Role Models Not Runway Models.™

Fox called it "The Runway Revolution" when she included powerful CEOs, executives, activists, and philanthropists on the runway instead of traditional models, including the first ever model on the runway in a wheelchair and the first ever model with Down Syndrome. Over 60 brands and advertising campaigns have emulated or have been inspired by Hammer's campaign.

Hammer, her line, and her movement have been featured on CNBC, Fox Business News, Forbes, Good Morning America, Elle, Marie Claire, Cosmopolitan among others. She studied Economics and Women's Studies at UCLA and Fashion Business and Marketing at the Parsons Paris School of Art and Design. Hammer is a graduate and recipient of the inaugural Tory Burch Goldman Sachs 10,000 Small Businesses program. She also holds a certificate in Fashion Law from the Fashion Law Institute at Fordham Law School.

Role Models Not Runway Models™ and Hammer appear under 'History' for New York Fashion Week in Wikipedia three times! Literally making beauty and fashion history.

CARRIE HAMMER
WWW.CARRIEHAMMER.COM

Carrie Hammer's customers are powerful women and executives. Carrie didn't feel comfortable sending teenage models down the runway to model her clothes and decided that she should present her brand to the market as Role Models Not Runway Models™. The decision was also primarily driven by a strong belief that the fashion industry wields a lot of clout and has a tremendous responsibility when it comes to young women's body image.

She felt her business model, and the way she designs and presents her clothing lines is an excellent opportunity to show young women that role models, not runway models, are who they should look up to.

Meet them here: http://carriehammer.tumblr.com/

Strength Can Come from Adversity and Difficult Beginnings

JODY HARRIS

"No matter the struggle, no matter the circumstances, never give up! Courage — Determination — Faith: Just think, if you find them today, where will your life be in the future?"
—JODY HARRIS

July 1985 was the hottest and muggiest there ever was in Oklahoma. A 16-year-old girl stood on her parent's front porch, knees shaking, bottom lip quivering, and heart beating so hard and loud it smothered the courage she kept trying to muster. She reached twice for the front door but couldn't pull it open. Her body language said she wanted to, and then it didn't. That emotional tug of war rocked her back and forth.

She had to tell her parents something no 16-year-old girl ever wants to say. She hadn't even said it aloud to herself yet. It was as if she did not mention it, then it would not be so. Her lips moved with just a mutter, rehearsing what she had to tell them. Reflex brought her hand off the door handle to cover her mouth. She prayed that somehow her parents, just inside sitting around the table, had not heard her.

The third try opened the door. The girl stepped inside, and they looked up at her. The lump in her throat moved enough for the words to come out without any preamble, "I'm pregnant." Their silence sent chills through her. She held her breath and braced for the worst. The blood rushed out of her father's face while her mother's face did the opposite, turning beet red as it locked squarely on her. And that made perfect sense. You see, she was daddy's girl, and her mother, a hard-working woman whose husband was on the road most of the time, had raised four children almost entirely on her own. Mother had always been the disciplinarian, the layer down of the law and her rule was harsh. Alone so often, her way of being strong was to never show any weakness and little forgiveness.

"What!" her mother stood so suddenly it nearly tipped the chair over as it went backward. Rage already tinged her scream. "That's a fine mess you've got yourself into." She shook her head in revulsion. The next words cut the girl to the bone. "Well, you're going to get an abortion, aren't you?"

The girl looked at her father. He hadn't moved, his face was still white as the tablecloth on the table he sat behind. She didn't look at her mother, instead searching her father's face for something, anything like compassion. In his eyes, she saw shock and hurt. Not looking away from him she replied to her mother, "I'm not having an abortion."

"Well, then you'll have to give--"

Now she looked at her and in that moment, seeing her mother's face contorted in anger and disgust, she discovered an inner resolve that hadn't existed minutes before—had not been inside that young girl shaking just outside the front door. She told her "I'm not giving my baby up." She looked at her father again. He had closed his eyes, his right hand wiped at the tears trickling down his cheeks. "I'm raising this baby." She told them.

The laughing snort came from her mother, "How are you going to do that?"

"I'll figure it out." That newfound resolve stiffened even further. "I'm going to give my baby the best life I can, and I will love it with all my heart."

Her mother stormed on, and the young girl stood there and took it until her father raised his head and with his bottom lip trembling said, "You really know how to hurt me."

Those words made the girl turn from them, and tears flowed down her face, dripping from her chin, as she walked out the back door. She vowed at that very moment to never give up and to always love unconditionally, no matter the circumstances. She would not be like her parents.

As the story unfolds, most of this girl's friends in school abandoned her one by one. When she walked through the halls, they turned the other way. They whispered behind her back. Their parents told their children not to associate with her. Everyone she loved made a point of telling her how she had disappointed them and had ruined her life.

By all accounts, this girl should have felt worthless. She had EVERY REASON to give up on herself. To become a victim. By all accounts, she should have felt hopeless, but didn't. Because something inside her, something she didn't realize was there—hidden maybe since birth, or maybe only until she opened that front door—blossomed in her. Faith, hope, and determination—to never give up and keep moving forward—wherever that came from, Lord knows she needed it. Lord knows it saved her.

Now, I know this girl—her story—very well, and I know what saved her. Because that girl was me.

I was brought up in a middle-class family. My dad worked and was gone most of the time. My mother was a housewife for most of my childhood. I was an average kid, good student, head cheerleader, and friend to everyone. I had met a boy five years older than me and thought I was in love. You know, like in the fairy tales you hear about, Romeo and Juliet—that kind of deep love. He said and did all the right things. I wasn't promiscuous but just knew what we had was so real that having sex with him seemed the right thing to do. As I just shared with you, it wasn't.

While my friends enjoyed their teenage years, I prepared for motherhood. While they prepared for college, I made a choice to be the best mother I could be and to work hard and never feel sorry for myself. I went on to have a baby girl, Jenilee, and marry the father. Over the next seven years, I welcomed two more precious children into my heart, my daughter, Randi Rae and my son Brice.

However, I hid a dark secret. I had married a violent and abusive man. As the violence grew, I feared for my safety and the safety of my children.

I remember being seven months pregnant with my third child, my son. Something had set my husband off, and I knew this time it was going to be bad. He dragged me by my hair into the bedroom where the gun cabinet was located and shoved me up against the wall.

"Stay! Don't you move." He turned from me to open a drawer and began shuffling through it. "Damn it."

He was looking for the keys to the cabinet. I silently prayed as he sorted through all the stuff that had accumulated in that drawer, shifting it around and cursing as he searched. If he found those keys and got a gun in his hand, I was likely dead.

I heard my daughters. They had learned not to be around him when he was hurting mommy and had stayed in their room as I had told them. But they were crying out, "Please don't hurt mommy!"

He slammed my head up against the gun cabinet. "You're a lucky woman today." He angrily gestured toward the hall and their bedroom. "Go shut them up!"

As I comforted them, my unborn son kicked and all I could think was, Lord I need to get away... got to get away. But being so far along with my pregnancy I was on leave from my job and didn't have any money. There was no way I would escape to my parent's house. My mind was so filled with worry and trying to figure out what to do, that I didn't sleep that night.

The next day, I found a paper route advertisement in the newspaper. I called—not telling them I was seven months pregnant—and found out the route was actually in my neighborhood. I got the job.

Every day, my daughters and I would roll and deliver the papers. Each week I took 75% of my paycheck and hid it in a new checking account that I had started. I gave my husband the other 25% and listened to him tell me how stupid I was for working for so little. After three and a half months of the paper route and going back to my regular job, I had accumulated enough to make a deposit and pay the first month's rent on an apartment.

Then came the hard part—the scary part—telling my husband I was leaving him. First, I had to get my daughters and son out of harm's way. My sister came and took them, and their packed bags, to her home so I could confront him. I knew I would either walk out, having escaped him, or I would die. Thank goodness, I am a survivor.

I was free. I didn't have much, but I had my kids, and that was my only priority. But I would not have even that if I had not stood up to my husband. And for that matter, to my parents years ago. I had learned to be strong, and that failure was not an option no matter my age, financial situation or the challenges—large and small—that life had dealt me. As a single mother of three, I was determined to never give up. If one door closed, I didn't stop. I kept knocking. When people told me I would never amount to anything, I did not listen and held my head up and kept moving forward. Determination, faith, and hope kept me alive and lead me to a successful career despite the challenges of not having a college degree and that early condemnation and public ridicule as a young, teenage mother.

When I was 18 years old and worked at the state treasurer's office, a woman named Vanda Wall saw potential in me and became a mentor. She taught me the importance of working hard, how to not bury myself in the past but to deal with the present and to always look ahead. She showed me that was the way to fix mistakes, and to always strive to learn more—to become more. Instrumental in teaching me the fundamentals of banking, her mentorship led me to two other mentors, officers in a bank, who also helped me. The senior vice president taught me how to read financial statements and prepare credit memos, how to argue my point in meetings, read people's actions and to stick to my instincts, which has been invaluable throughout my career. The president of the bank gave me confidence and told me: "You can be anything you want to be."

I needed that kind of inspiration because as a very young woman—and a single mother—working in a financial institution I was ripe for gossip and behind my back commentary. Because I had young children in daycare, two of them latch-key kids which meant they went home after school and were alone until I got off work, these women were brutal in their judgment of me. One female co-worker told me to my face, "You should quit your job and live off welfare." She had a condescending, mean, look on her face as she said, "that's where you belong," before she turned dismissively away. That comment still inspires me to this day, to work hard and let the quality of what I do speak for itself.

Since those early days, I have had several amazing mentors. They have inspired me, been great sounding boards and when I wanted to stop or give up, they reminded me that what I was working for was important: to show other women that it doesn't matter where you came from, where you have been or what you have done... you can be anything you set a goal for and work toward.

Years passed, my children grew, and I established myself as a competent professional and had positions of increasing responsibility. I was traveling on business when something happened that became a turning point in my adult life. One morning, I was determined to wear my favorite dress. It zipped in the back—every woman has struggled with this at one time or another—and I could not get it zipped. I had tried everything, almost dislocating my arms and shoulders in the process, and nothing worked. I looked in the mirror and saw a distressed, desperate woman who was running late for an important business meeting. I called the hotel's concierge desk, and when I hung up I thought, that was an interesting conversation. I'm sure it will show up as a skit on a late-night television show one of these days. The clock was ticking, it was getting later and later, as I walked out in the hallway determined to find someone to help me. I had asked several possible prospects with no takers. They looked at me like I was crazy and kept moving, maybe a little quicker than normal, away from me. I was standing there, in the hallway outside of my room, when a mature gentleman came from his room a few doors from mine and noticed me. He smiled and said: "I bet you need help getting zipped."

I was so thankful and returned his smile, "Yes, please!"

As he zipped me, he commented, "If someone invented something to zip these dresses, they would get rich."

I had never designed anything in my life, but at that moment something—a part of me—ignited the idea that would become that product.

A week later, I arrived home and shared my damsel in distress story with my family. "Mom, you didn't let some stranger zip up your dress!" My family was mortified.

"I had no choice, but you know what?" They all looked at me. "I'm going to solve that problem, so other women won't have to rely on anyone like I had to."

* * *

For me, the process of creating a product (and it could work for a service, too) begins with trying to solve a problem. I must analyze it from all angles and ask questions, such as why is it a problem? When does it become one? Where is the problem and how does it show up? As I reviewed my responses, I saw a common denominator. If I can't zip up my dress by myself, how do people with mobility issues get zipped up or how does a handicapped person with one arm get zipped up? Then I asked myself, when do people encounter these problems? In a hotel? Away on business? At home, wanting to surprise their significant other with being dressed on time? Or just getting dressed by themselves for church on Sunday morning? The answers I came up with revealed to me that the product needed to be compact, easily accessible and fashionable. Now that I had a vision of it I went to work.

First, I started out with a simple rough drawing of what I imagined the product to look like. Then went to local hardware and craft stores to purchase the components of the product. Shopping for them was not easy. I still can see the perplexed faces of those store employees as I explained what I wanted when in some ways, I wasn't sure myself. There was a lot of trial and error. Next, I needed to build a prototype. Then I had to decorate my prototype, so it was appealing to the consumer.

One of my biggest fears was the prototype not working when I demonstrated it. My first ZippedMe was a simple, yet functional product. I was so excited because it solved one problem, it zipped up my dress. But what about the other problems I had discovered during the development process? How would it help a person with mobility issues or a handicapped person with one arm? Also, did it look fashionable? If I was in a hurry could I wear it as a necklace?

Reluctantly, I went back to the drawing board. I admit this was a challenge for me. I didn't like demolishing and recreating my ZippedMe. But I knew without a doubt it had to be functional and solve ALL the identified problems. Days turned into weeks. Weeks turned into months. Iteration after iteration until finally, I had created the ZippedMe that covered it all. And this problem-solving accessory was more than I could have ever imagined.

Soon after I invented my product, a few of my friends started asking me to make them one because they struggled to get zipped up for work or for church. A month or two later another friend asked me where she could buy more. She wanted to give them away as Christmas presents. After thinking it over, I realized that if my friends wanted to buy a few ZippedMes, how many other people would want to buy them for their girlfriends, or as Christmas or birthday gifts? I remember sitting in my office holding my invention and saying half-aloud to myself, 'this little problem-solving product just transformed into a real business.'

Now things got serious. I spent months filing legal documents for the business, buying components for inventory, putting together a manufacturing team and hiring my nephew Matt Lee's company, Lead

Generation Experts, to create my website. Then in March 2014, I officially launched ZippedMe, and my life has never been the same.

Each day since starting this journey, I am thankful and feel blessed because ZippedMe has created opportunities for my community and my family. It has allowed me to come full circle by helping people help themselves. And more importantly, it has opened my mind to thinking about all the things we encounter that we find a hassle or a full-blown problem. Or even, disgusting.

I constantly travel through airports or attend public events such as concerts, sporting venues, BBQ contests, etc. So, I often must use public restrooms—have you seen many of them!—and finally had to draw a line and say, "NO MORE" at the condition of toilet seats I was forced to use or avoid (then endure the discomfort of holding it) until I got to a cleaner facility. Just as ZippedMe had been an invention of necessity, so too would be my next product.

I began formulating my latest problem-solving solution, YukBGone, in February 2015 and had two goals in mind: a travel-sized product that would clean a toilet seat, and be nontoxic. After a couple of months, I finally came up with a formula that both cleaned and deodorized but did not include any of nineteen ingredients banned by the Food and Drug Administration (FDA).

In May of 2015, YukBGone was introduced to the marketplace and is available in boutiques, small local grocers, at Amazon.com and has been accepted to sell on WalMart.com. YukBGone has been certified by an FDA lab as safe, nontoxic and effective and since receiving this certification, sales and visibility have skyrocketed.

I've learned so much about myself, mostly that being strong and believing if I keep working, keep trying... that I can accomplish many things and get from life what I want. But—and I tell this to people who ask me for advice—first, you are going to make a lot of mistakes when starting out. I made several when I started my business. However, the lessons I learned were instrumental in making my business successful.

I thought if I created a useful, problem-solving, accessory that customers would come out of the woodwork and line up to buy my ZippedMes. But that wasn't the case in the beginning. I had to learn to build a relationship with my customers and discover why they wanted my product, which gave me a foundation for how to market it. Once I learned this lesson, my passion, dedication, and hope for the product came alive.

Another lesson I've learned is that first and foremost, we should all take a little time and look at how far we have come on our journey in life. This step has always been crucial to me because if I hadn't taken it—that self-reflection—I could have and likely would have gotten discouraged, thinking I was not getting anywhere. When I was, but incrementally. Tiny steps can get you where you want to go, but you must take them each and every day.

When you take your product or business to the next level, your resilience will be tested by adversity. When I started marketing ZippedMe, it was hard to understand that some people didn't want an accessory that solved a problem just because it existed. I had to realize that most of my customers had to hear about my product at least eight times before they discovered that they needed it. With that realization, I began promoting ZippedMe through different sources like social media, advertising in magazines, guest appearances, product showcases and participating in podcast and radio talk shows. All these means of gaining visibility have been a major part of my success:

Social media—a must-have resource and tool that can catapult a business into profitability. You should use it to build momentum and, though the results don't happen as consistently as you hope, you will increase your potential for success.

Branding—with the right content and effort, you can build a reputation for your brand around your company's message and offerings.

Community—you can develop and cultivate a neighborhood where your customers will emotionally connect with you, and you have an opportunity to establish a valuable dialogue with them. This type of connection is stronger than paid market research.

Impact—as you build your network, your influence increases. Once you have a significant social media audience, you develop a snowball effect that will draw in new customers, media opportunities and collaboration with partners.

Website traffic—your social media effort can lead to increased traffic on your site. By sharing posts, special sales, and videos, you can generate visitors to your site. You can monitor this by utilizing resources such as the one I personally use, Google Analytics. It's free to install and implement and generates detailed statistics about the visitors to my site. It also measures conversion from my social media activities, showing how effective it is in driving people to my site.

Here are three things that I wish I had known when I started my company. Take it as good advice from someone who has been in the trenches:

1. Personal Development is critical to the success of your business.
2. Technology changes rapidly, therefore, stay ahead of the curve or hire someone who will oversee keeping you current.
3. Mentors are a game changer and best-kept secret in the success of your business.

But all the mistakes I made with ZippedMe were lessons learned which made the launch of my latest product, YukBGone, much easier.

I'll close my chapter with this: I will never forget a lady calling a couple weeks after purchasing a ZippedMe at a show. When I answered the phone, I had no idea how memorable it would:

"I wanted to thank you," the women replied when I picked up her call. "My daughter was born with only one arm…" I could hear the catch in her voice, the kind you get when you want to say something but emotion chokes you. "She loves fashion, dresses and such, but always had to ask for help when she wore them." The women paused. "And that was always a reminder of her disability as if she needed something else to do that." Then her tone lightened, "Thank you for creating something that helps her feel independent."

When I hung up the phone, tears streamed down my face. As I sat on the floor replaying the phone call in my mind, I told myself, 'if I sell one ZippedMe or ten thousand… I will never forget the impact one of my inventions is making in people's lives.'

To me, success means to give more than you receive. Live your life free of fear and full of passion for making your dreams a reality. And when someone needs a helping hand… help them. I measure my success by my heart and soul... when they are full from helping others live out their dream and providing problem-solving products, then I know I am successful.

About Jody Harris

At 16, Jody found herself pregnant and that everyone had turned their back on her. She was told to stay away from her friends because their parents did not approve. On her own, while those friends enjoyed their teenage years, Jody became a mother. At that point, she made a choice to be the best mother she could and to work hard and never feel sorry for herself. Overcoming the mistakes of youth and an abusive, life-threatening marriage, Jody Harris is now an award-winning inventor, bestselling author, bestselling publisher, highly regarded speaker, a grandmother, and successful business woman.

Jody Harris Inc.
WWW.JODYHARRISINC.COM

Jody Harris Inc. is a solution-based company whose CEO and Founder invented the award-winning

ZippedMe and the multi-award-winning YukBGone to solve everyday problems. Her desire and passion of giving women a voice led her to launch a publishing company, Symphony Publishing. Her down to Earth—storyteller's—approach to speaking has made her a sought after motivational speaker which has landed her at major events and stages.

Leaving a Dark Past Behind to Create a Bright Present and Future

CYNTHIA JAMIN

"Every day is a new day, and you'll never be able to find happiness if you don't move on."

–CARRIE UNDERWOOD

Sometimes you just know when it's time to move on. I knew it was time for me when I started resenting the fact I had to take a shower and get ready to go to an audition. I was a television actress and had appeared on numerous shows (*Seinfeld, Just Shoot Me, ER, Will & Grace, Suddenly Susan, Veronica's Closet* and many others). I was also on *Friends;* I started on the pilot, and then they brought me back to play Jasmine, a recurring character on this iconic sitcom.

After enjoying some success, I felt I was in a prime position to get cast as a regular on a sitcom. But more and more, those breaks eluded me. The industry began hiring 'name' actors, and those of us who had paid our dues but were not 'names,' were overlooked.

Even though I had achieved a lot as an actress, I was frustrated with having to wait for chances to do what I love. So, I decided to go to college and see what other opportunities might be out there. Already in my 30s, going to college for the first time was a daunting adventure, and it took me three and a half years to get a two-year associates degree. During this period, I still worked as an actress and an assistant to a writer to pay the bills. Everything was going as planned until I was cast on an episode of *Just Shoot Me*. Little did I know that it would change my life forever.

And not because of what you think. I wasn't offered a series regular role, nope. Something much better, I met my soul mate... Michael Jamin, a staff writer on the show. Three years later we got married and had our first daughter Roxy, and then Lola a couple of years later. For the first time since I was 17, I was fortunate to not have to work. I could concentrate on raising our two daughters. I'm so grateful I had that time with them!

One day, I was with my mother, and she told me, "We should take this sewing class together."

Now, I'm not a very crafty person. I don't draw, paint or anything like that. "What do you mean?"

"Your grandmother used to make you clothes and costumes, don't you remember? Let's try it!"

We took the class, and I was surprised at how much I loved the instant gratification from something as simple as sewing (though some projects can be complex, as I soon learned). The minute I was done with a project it could be used immediately. I didn't have to depend on anyone else to get it done for me (like with an agent finding me work) or give me the chance to do it (running to auditions and hoping they'd pick me). It was pure creative freedom, and the immediacy of the result was intoxicating.

After starting with the basics, pillows, curtains, etc., I was eager to make clothing for my two daughters. I started with fun little skirts, pants, and dresses. Then a friend of mine asked if I would make a custom flower-girl dress. As I was sewing it with my teacher, I was amazed at all the work that went into the lining. The inside of the dress was as pretty as the outside, but no one would see that... after all, it's just lining.

I had tried to find a dress for my daughters that was something they would want to wear all the time. And it had to be unique enough to play pretend in and feel beautiful wearing. And of course, it had to be comfortable enough to wear every day, too! That's a lot to ask of one dress, and as hard as I looked, it didn't exist in the marketplace. That flower-girl dress design would be perfect for my girls, and I decided to remake it. Because my kids can't stand it when clothes are scratchy, I figured out how to hide the seams away from their bodies. And fortunately, I live near the Los Angeles Fashion District, so finding amazingly soft and fun fabric wasn't hard. Seriously, I found the best fabrics ever! Every time I go on buying sprees, I'm like a kid in a candy store.

I came up with a design for a really cute reversible dress, and it was TWIRLY (what's the point of wearing a dress if it doesn't twirl)! The minute that dress was finished, the girls wouldn't take it off. It was exactly what I had searched for and not been able to find. And the Original Reversible Twirly Dress® was born!

Original Reversible Twirly Dress

There was only the one dress at that moment, so they had to share. After many fights over who could wear it, I quickly made more. That's when I knew it was something exceptional. The girls had never reacted to any clothing quite like that. It was magical.

The dresses were such a big hit at their school that several mothers approached me about creating twirly dresses for their girls. That's when my hobby became my new profession, and TwirlyGirl was created.

I didn't start manufacturing my design right away and instead, took an Apparel Construction class at Otis School of Design to learn about this new—to me—industry. I wasn't planning on finishing a degree but wanted to have a little more knowledge before investing in this new adventure. I didn't know how to proceed with TwirlyGirl but knew I was onto something worth pursuing. My Apparel Construction teacher helped draft the first production pattern of my Original Reversible Twirly Dress.

At first, I sewed everything in my dining room and worked out of my house. When a local children's fashion boutique heard about our dresses, they wanted them too, and I simply couldn't keep up with demand.

My teacher then referred me to a local cutter and sewer, and that's how I started manufacturing. Soon I needed more help—to add other styles—and was lucky that other contractors wanted to work with me right out of the gate, with no experience. It's not easy finding those that will work with small quantities and charge you a fair price. At first, I had to train them about how I wanted everything sewn. That part was a little weird because I didn't have nearly as much sewing experience as they had and yet I was correcting them. But I wanted it done exactly right, even if it cost more.

I still worked out of my house after production was underway (then and now, I choose to outsource all the work to local contractors). I didn't take on the cost of an office until two years later when there just wasn't room in my house anymore. The office is downtown and where we handle our customer service and house all our inventory. It also serves as our showroom and shipping headquarters.

Moving into my new office felt like the most triumphant moment. It meant I was really doing this... I had founded a business on nothing but an idea! There was a different level of commitment, and it clearly was no longer a hobby. It felt great to have my own space and for TwirlyGirl to be standing on her own.

And now that I had an office, I needed a little more help. I was lucky enough to find Heather, a recent graduate of the prestigious FIDM (Fashion Institute of Design and Merchandising in Los Angeles). Heather not only helped run the front office, from shipping to customer service but also contributed designs for new styles. I had all I needed to go full steam ahead.

TwirlyGirl grew very slowly, and I'm glad that I took my time to get to know the business and my customers. It was crucial that TwirlyGirl continued to be self-funded. No loans, no debt, no second mortgage on the house. I didn't want that kind of financial pressure. That's still the same today.

As business grew, more opportunities came our way. One day, a little girl walked into Nordstrom wearing her TwirlyGirl dress, and it caught the eye of one of their buyers. The buyer got our information and immediately called to place an initial order

Getting access to department store buyers is a very hard thing to do, even at industry trade shows. There are so many gatekeepers between clothing manufacturers—especially small companies like mine—and the actual buyer that it's almost impossible to get through to them directly. A girl wearing one of our dresses catching the eye of a Nordstrom buyer, who then contacted us directly... was a huge moment. Their order was already a done deal. They wouldn't have contacted us if they were not interested. So, the call was mainly working out the terms and the details. That willingness for them to initiate the contact to work with us in any way to get our product in their stores was the best position for a company like mine. Because we didn't seek them out, we got to call the shots.

I decided to send them an assortment of our dresses. Which means they didn't just get twenty pink, or twenty purple or twenty orange... they got an assortment of prints that I thought would sell. That first order sold out quickly.

Nordstrom was shocked. They didn't think it was going to sell through so fast. The buyer called me back. "I want to reorder... but here's the problem." This was when things started to change, where I had less control. She continued, "I want to order quickly, but it can't be assorted dresses or SKUs."

"What do you mean?" I asked

"It's really about logistics. Our systems aren't designed to handle one-of-a-kind products."

Which is what TwirlyGirl dresses are all about, a one-of-a-kind appeal. The reason the first order sold out so quickly, was because they didn't see 50 of the same dress. They saw one or two that were similar, but all were different. I started to see the problem.

"When we order in volume if one store runs out of a size, we need to move it from one store to another, easily... we can't do this with your products—not the way the last order came to us."

I understood her. How we produced dresses and delivered them did not match up with their internal system and their need to be able to transfer inventory from one store to the next.

The Nordstrom buyer explained further, "We can only order and bring in two or three of your SKUs. And we must know exactly what they are, what colors, what sizes you are sending us. And I need to actually select which ones we want so that I know precisely what we're getting."

"Let me call you back." I needed to think through what she had told me meant. My first reaction was being happy that the first order sold well, but this second order was shaping up to be much different. I thought about our conversation, then called and left a message for the buyer, "Let's wait and do things with the proper timing and be ready for spring."

They called me back, "You don't get many opportunities like this. This is going to be a nice size order for you."

I saw the writing on the wall. If I wanted Nordstrom's business, I had to do what they said. At the time, I didn't know any different. I felt I couldn't turn the business away. We worked hard to fill their second order exactly the way that they wanted. It took longer and required more lead time. In my gut, I knew taking that order under their terms and conditions was a wrong decision. Because of the timing, I knew they were bringing it in too late. They brought it in for July, late in the summer season, with only two weeks to sell and clear the way for fall merchandise in August.

What happened was exactly what I thought would happen. The second order didn't sell through, and Nordstrom blamed it on the product—my dresses. They didn't blame it on the buyer who brought it in too late and limited the selection to their customers. That was pretty much the end with Nordstrom. Or so I thought. The funny thing is about two years after that, they called me to order again. They did the same thing because they had $10,000 extra in their budget. And ended up with the same result, because of the timing and their choices, the product did not sell through. Even though I knew that fulfilling their order would result in the same outcome, I wasn't going to turn down $10,000. I didn't expect them to come back after that first round, so I wasn't counting on further business anyway.

This experience with Nordstrom proved to me that department store buyers may want my products, but they can't sell them the way they need to be sold. And it was purely a technical issue. Because if it would've worked within their system—or if they were willing to change—TwirlyGirl would have been a huge hit for them. But changing their system for one supplier was out of the question. It makes you wonder how much better department store offerings would be if they could work with smaller manufacturers.

There were other considerations, too. Department stores and big-box retailers (like Walmart, Target, etc.) require steep discounts along with very strict packing guidelines... at least a hundred pages of instructions! And if you don't do it right, they fine you. To make selling to those types of wholesale buyers profitable, we would have to bring down our costs significantly. That meant outsourcing our sewing overseas, where labor costs can be much less. But manufacturing overseas carries with it another set of risks. You can't see if something is being done wrong, it's hard to oversee working conditions of the employees, and shipping takes considerably longer. By the time you receive your goods and inspect them, it's too late to send anything back, that isn't done correctly. So, you spend more money fixing it, here in the States. I found out that there are contractors that only repair garments from overseas. In the industry, they are—appropriately—called 'fixers.' You know that if there's a group of known and named skilled people that can make a living doing that, it must happen a LOT!

My decision to keep everything made in Los Angeles was easy and twofold: First, the exploitation of workers—rampant in the clothing industry—was out of the question. I'm sure there are factories overseas where the workers are treated well, but how would I know for sure? And second, TwirlyGirl garments are very complicated to sew. With so many contrasting fabrics, it's easy for things to go wrong. I'm extremely picky on how our clothes are sewn. I insist on using the highest quality stitching, and I want all the seams tucked away. Outsourcing overseas meant I would lose control over this process. I would keep the 'Fixers' very busy, and that would eat up profits!

But, if we wanted to play with in the big leagues—get into the big-box high-volume retailers—that is what it would take.

I was at a crossroads. What kind of business did I want to become? This looped back around to the wholesale versus direct to the customer debate. To scale the business to cater to high-volume wholesale buyers, we'd have to basically become a commodity business (to the buyers and internally from a production standpoint). I did not want that and felt it would devalue not only what had accomplished so far, but also the product.

After much hand-wringing, I decided to scale back and not pursue the big wholesale accounts. I wanted to stay faithful to our values and cater directly to my customers and small boutiques. This would allow me to focus all my resources on making high-quality garments and providing excellent customer service. That's why I'm so proud of the many glowing reviews that our customers write. Plus, I LOVE the idea of manufacturing locally. It's good for our economy, and it's the right thing to do.

We have managed to work out things with our smaller boutiques because they're more flexible. We even offer an exchange program where if some sizes or colors are not selling as fast, we trade them for something else in our line. That way the retailers we develop relationships with never feel like they're stuck with something. This policy is very rare in the industry, most clothing manufacturers would never dream of doing this. We believe in helping our retailers be successful, and because we are not a typical clothing line, we can offer this courtesy.

I also refuse to have running sales. Unlike most manufacturers offering daily deals, we only have two sales a year. Our sales include discontinued styles and

Perfectly Imperfect (PIPS) garments. These have slight flaws, and we can't sell them at regular prices. Our Bi-Annual Blowouts are amazingly popular because our customers know that they're not going to be able to get these steeply discounted items year-round.

Most clothing lines can't do this and that makes us more valuable, not a commodity product, which helps protect our pricing. This also instills loyalty with our customers and our retailers.

We create that unique dress every girl remembers forever. This one sentence informs every decision I make. I regularly ask myself, will this style make our clothing more or less memorable? AND will she—our customer—want to wear it all the time? That's super important to me.

My husband, Michael has always been incredibly supportive, always encouraging me to do what I wanted to do with the business. When I first started, he was heavily involved with his own career as a sitcom writer. And I didn't think I needed him to do anything, after all, he knew as much about business as I did, which was nothing. For the first seven years, Michael was on the sidelines, watching all the twists and turns and not saying much. Heather and I did it all.

Around year five, I brought in a woman who had a ton of experience growing businesses. We wanted to see if we could penetrate the wholesale market more than we had at the time. After about a year, it was clear we weren't doing much better, so we parted ways. I'm still great friends with her and wouldn't have traded that time for anything. It was a tremendous learning experience for us.

Around year six, my father, being an entrepreneur, wanted to see if he could contribute to the business and attempt to grow our wholesale market again, but from another angle. After about a year, that also didn't work out, and thankfully, we are still very close! It's always risky to involve family... I've only had positive experiences so far.

This was when Michael started to take more interest. He saw, from the outside, what we had tried that didn't work. He wasn't in the trenches or attached to a plan, idea or a 'promise of increasing our wholesale business.' Instead, he saw things clearly and contributed insight about the direction we should be heading: focusing on selling directly to our customer. It was crystal clear, once he pointed it out. Our own numbers showed that wholesale was not our path, our retail orders had grown year over year without us doing anything. Imagine if we had invested all those resources allocated for wholesale, and switched it to gaining direct retail customers. What a difference that could make! And it did.

Michael dove in head first and hasn't looked back since. He taught himself everything he needed to know about online marketing, from email automation to Facebook ads, to how to optimize a website. His creative writing skills have helped our brand in a big way. He is responsible for creating a complete TwirlyGirl world, full of stories for every style. Even the outreach to our customers, from personalized emails and order confirmations to the hang tag, has something to delight the customer. Our website is full of Michael's creative touches. He still works at his day job, but as an integral part of TwirlyGirl, he's found a new passion in designing his own future.

I also began to expand my knowledge and started helping with the graphics, getting involved in every aspect of the site, SEO, email marketing, QuickBooks (knowing the numbers is so important for pricing items correctly), etc.

Michael and I both love being entrepreneurs.

***

But don't little girls grow up?

That question created another decision point for our business. TwirlyGirl was originally created for our daughters, Roxy and Lola. In fact, if you look carefully enough you'll see old photos of them wearing TwirlyGirl throughout our website. For years, they both proudly wore our clothes everywhere. Imagine our horror when Roxy, age 14, announced she was too old to wear TwirlyGirl (the biggest size for our clothing is 14). As her tastes matured, she wanted more subdued colors and sophisticated styles. Whereas in the past, she could just go to our showroom and pick something out, now she was spending hours in the mall fruitlessly searching for clothes that reflected her style. The truth is, the Junior segment is significantly underrepresented in stores. Teenagers are being marketed to as if they are women, and they're not. Their tastes are different, and their bodies are different.

Fortunately, Roxy is an art student at the renowned Los Angeles County High School for the Arts (LACHSA). We asked her what she would like to wear, and Roxy grabbed a pencil and began sketching. She was drawn to classic silhouettes with a slightly retro flair. We were so impressed, we encouraged Roxy to put her styles into production. But as parents, we wouldn't be holding her hand. We'd supervise her, give her pointers but ultimately, this was going to be her project.

Roxy jumped right in. She was intimately involved in the pattern making, cutting, grading, and marketing of her new line. She styled the photoshoot and instructed our photographer on the look she wanted. Roxy named her new line 'Jam & Bread,' a play on our last name, Jamin. She started with five styles: a chic reversible lace up dress, a retro teen romper, a bohemian jumpsuit, a classic full circle skirt that's reversible, and of course, a new twist on our Original Reversible Twirly Dress®. Jam & Bread is perfect for the girls who love something different, grew up with TwirlyGirl, and can't find anything out there that feels right for them.

Since we were creating for the teens, I felt the need to dip a toe into the women's arena. We hear women say this to us all the time, "I wish that was in my size!" and we have done our best to make styles that crossover. We now have TwirlyGirl styles for women. It's time for us ladies to start twirling!

In 2006, I created that first Original Reversible Twirly Dress®, and today I'm the owner of a thriving business. I'm so proud to say that we have sold tens of thousands of dresses on our website and in specialty children's boutiques and gift stores across the United States and Canada. Everyone at TwirlyGirl is treated like family... including our customers. No one leaves without a smile on their face.

In 2015, we had 75% of our sales come from our website and 25% from wholesale. Selling directly to our customer allows us to be much more profitable. We still contract out all our sewing and cutting to local contractors in the Los Angeles area. We continue to buy all our fabrics and materials locally.

We still take risks. It's never a given that last year's sales will be the same or more than the previous year. It sounds obvious to think this, but you would be surprised at how easy it is to get lulled into complacency. We must keep moving, growing, and expand our reach. Just when you think you have exhausted every avenue, there is usually something else you can try, and definitely, always more to improve upon. We never stop tweaking our messaging and our website, constantly looking for that right phrase and functionality.

In addition to all the external changes the business has brought into my life, TwirlyGirl has affected me internally—personally—in a very profound way. I've carried a very dark secret with me my whole life and during my journey of building this business. And it's become evident what has motivated (and still drives) me—not the money, or even being an entrepreneur—though it is something I would never have expected: a need to reclaim what was taken from me.

I came from an abusive childhood. I grew up the only child of a poor single mother who, because of her own demons, couldn't give me the attention that every child deserves.

When I was seven, a man offered to let me attend his sleep away camp for free. This is me on my first day.

Look at how happy I was. But why would a grown man, a complete stranger, take such an interest in a little girl he didn't know? Because he knew I would make the perfect victim.

For the next six years, I was abused by him. This is me on the last day of camp that first summer. It would take years before I got my smile back.

I didn't realize this when I started TwirlyGirl years ago, but it's obvious to me now. When I go to work, every day I'm not just creating girls' clothing. I'm creating the childhood I never had. As a girl, I never felt carefree enough to twirl around in a pretty dress. Never. The abuse took that away. I felt ashamed, ugly... invisible and unworthy of feeling that much joy.

TwirlyGirl helped me find who I was again because every day I play a small part in creating moments of pure childhood innocence. A moment that a girl enjoys just for herself and not for anyone else. A twirl.

This is the meaning I have created from my horrible past. It doesn't fix it, but it does give it value. Today, I design girls' clothing and what I do fills me with joy. I believe it's the same joy that girls get wearing TwirlyGirl.

Of the many things, I have learned, one thing that has stuck with me every day: Always remember why I'm doing this. I believe in creating something girls treasure, to be a part of their childhood, making it unique in a memorable, extraordinary way. I want every customer to feel like they are our only one. And I want them to know how much I appreciate them. When I lose sight of this and get bogged down in the numbers or the unknown, I start to fret and fear the future. But my truth and my passion ground me and allow me to find the determination to continue.

Running a business is teaching me so much, every single day. I am so grateful that I could go on this journey and make it this far. I look forward to the possibilities and sharing all the joy I can.

When I think of what success means, there are two parts, professional and personal. Professionally, customer satisfaction is most important. If my customers are happy, they will tell their friends and keep coming back. It's how my business grows. We also set goals for our company, and we strategically plan to reach those goals. When a milestone is reached, it's time for a mini-celebration.

Personally, I ask myself: 'Am I fulfilled?' If I'm challenged creatively and learning, growing, excited about waking up in the morning, and looking forward to what the day will bring, then I'm fulfilled and grateful. I also ask myself if I'm the best person I can be in any given situation. Am I giving off positive vibes? Am I taking responsibility for my impact on others? Am I the best wife, mother, friend, business associate, boss, neighbor, stranger, etc.? When my head hits the pillow, and I can say I feel good about how the day went overall, then that's success.

ABOUT CYNTHIA JAMIN

Cynthia grew up in Chicago. Because of childhood abuse, she relocated to California to live with her father. Even though she attended Beverly Hills High School, Cynthia hardly came from privilege.

Just like in the movie *Slums of Beverly Hills*, her father rented a small apartment in the school district so that Cynthia could attend a great public high school. They put a bed in the dining room and made it her bedroom. Upon graduation, Cynthia became a professional dancer in music videos. Later, she became an actress and fell in love with Michael Jamin, a staff writer on the show, *Just Shoot Me*. An atypical Hollywood love story, Cynthia, and Michael have been happily married since May 2000, and have two daughters: Roxy and Lola. As the girls got older, Cynthia had trouble finding dresses they wanted to wear. Either they weren't colorful enough, or comfortable enough. Taking matters into her own hands, Cynthia took sewing lessons. Her first creation was a reversible twirly dress that was super comfortable. All the itchy seams were tucked away from their bodies, and the fabrics were vibrant and full of joy. Her daughters loved them. Soon other moms were asking where they could get one of these twirly dresses for their own girls.

In 2006, with a $20,000 inheritance and a lot of hard work, a business was born!

TwirlyGirl
WWW.TWIRLYGIRLSHOP.COM

TwirlyGirl is now a million-dollar brand found in boutiques across the U.S., Canada, and Europe as well as on their website.

They specialize in creating that special dress that girls will remember forever. Everything is unique, super soft, and, of course, twirly.

They continue to expand their reach by selling directly to the consumer on their website and are in early talks to open a TwirlyGirl flagship brick and mortar store. It's truly a family business that has reaped rewards never dreamed of.

The Importance of Authenticity

ERIN JANKLOW

"Anyone who has never made a mistake has never tried anything new."
—ALBERT EINSTEIN

Following my curiosity for new experiences, I moved to Rome, Italy in 2009 to pursue a goal I had set as an undergraduate—despite having no single prior contact in the city. I had limited knowledge of modern-day Rome, proving yet again the impracticality of my undergraduate degree in Comparative Ancient History.

This was shortly after graduating from Northwestern University in 2008 at the peak of the financial crisis. To me, my degree and studies were *supremely* fascinating—though it was not the most marketable or tangible skill set. I knew that my 'dream job' in the States would be hard to come by during an economic downturn. Equally, I felt that pursuing my passion for the Italian language, while living in Italy, would enable me to learn and grow in ways that I could not yet define or imagine.

I anticipated that a blind move would be challenging, and optimistically framed my mindset to prepare for an undoubtedly challenging 3-6 months of 'newness.' Within two weeks I had my first (of many) apartments, jobs, and friends. Everything simply continued to improve, and I decided to stay! I had no idea how much I was taking on when, as a 23-year-old, I arrived at the Leonardo da Vinci–Fiumicino Airport with two massive suitcases. Now, no challenge seems daunting in comparison! This mindset has helped me immensely when starting my business.

Before I moved to Rome, I had a brief exposure to the Italian way of life. In college, I studied abroad in Bologna, Italy, which began my lifelong love affair with the country. Despite studying Italian for two years, I arrived as one of the weakest language speakers in the group—and language is not a skill you can fake! I realized within my first week the hard work ahead of me and resolved to do everything possible to converse with the people in the city where I would live for several months. I leaned heavily on my friends with more advanced language skills, and from them learned many explanations and rationale that reduced my confusion with the tongue.

I was fortunate to find an apartment with incredible housemates. They were exceedingly kind, patient, outgoing and generous. By observing their mannerisms and interactions, I could tell within minutes that we would become close friends if only I could communicate better. My goal quickly became to win them over by the time I left. Having a clear goal and consistent reinforcement was crucial to keeping my motivation high, and to achieving my ultimate success with the Italian language.

With persistence, uncountable flashcards, many Disney movies in Italian, a near soul shattering voyage to IKEA, and multiple language errors, I brought my fledgling language skills from beginner to advanced in a six-month period.

Learning details of new cultures is my favorite way to expand my views and look past cultural biases, and the Italians continually inspired me. My focus on developing basic language skills had delayed me from, yet prepared me for, truly understanding Italy's intricacies. I realized just before returning to the United States that I was on the cusp of grasping how Italian culture worked. I was eager to go back to Italy to further expand my understanding. Moving to Rome after graduation became my goal halfway through my time abroad. I told my family and friends, and it simply became 'the plan.'

I recall adults in my life fondly discussing their respective times abroad, sighing and saying wistfully: "Oh, I wish I could go back; Living abroad was the best four months of my life…" I remember thinking: 'Well, I feel this way too,' and saw returning as the most logical decision for MY long-term happiness without regrets.

A few months after graduation, the ever-mindreading universe (or creepy tech algorithms) helped me when Gmail popped up an ad for a supremely discounted one-way ticket to Rome. I took that to be a clear sign, bought the ticket that day, and left one month later. In doing so, I made good on the statement I had made to friends, family, and most importantly, myself. Taking the leap and committing is far more rewarding than perpetuating an eternal daydream.

* * *

Born and raised in Colorado, I've got sunshine in my bones! Creative, curious, and compassionate, I strive to see everyone and everything in its best light. I was brought up in an agricultural town and am therefore acutely aware of communication challenges between Americans, new, old, and undocumented. I assumed learning a language as an adult was next to impossible after observing how hard all members of my community worked. Perhaps that was a part of what formed my interest in languages and cultures. After a charmed childhood (Straight-A student, National Dance Team Champion, Sutdent Body Pres *and* Homecoming Queen... but I'm not living in the past, I promise!), I spread my wings to explore. My first stop, as mentioned, was Northwestern, where I studied, froze, and danced on the varsity dance team before joining a social and swing dance group. This paved the way for my four-year-stint living 'la bella vita' in Italy, where I became completely fluent in Italian, made time to appreciate small details, and learned the intricacies of Italian cooking (and eating)!

I did not know at the time that in my decision to move to Rome, and all the practical experience gained by my commitment to becoming fluent in Italian, I was watering a hidden seed of an idea. When I returned to the United States to acquire my MBA, I learned about social enterprise, which brought that seed to life. I discovered a profitable and scalable model to empower individuals around the world to develop language skills, which is critical for effective communication.

I am fortunate to have an incredibly supportive web of family, friends, and mentors. Some of my biggest role models are of course my immediate family. My mom, dad, and sister provide unconditional love and support. Our close relationships allow my strongest supporters to highlight the bigger picture of challenges that I face and ultimately help me to put forth my best possible work at all times. My grandmother, too, is ever inspiring. She was the first female interior designer hired by a prestigious Chicago firm and worked to bring more women into the company and the field. Always bright-eyed and dressed in bold colors, she is an incredible example of working hard, creating opportunities and staying faithful to your values. Additional mentors range across the board from peers in shared co-working spaces to previous bosses to professors and faculty from Babson College and the WIN (Women Innovating Now) Lab. Observing other successful women keeps me thinking big. Life and business can sometimes feel like the big unknown. Learning from women who have navigated the road before me gives me confidence and helps me envision opportunities which I can then create.

A network of support and inspiration—be it from family, friends, or peers—is perhaps most needed when encountering one thing that women face in both personal lives and in business: Sexism. We've come a long way in creating equal opportunities for women, yet we still have a ways to go to shift our cultural mindset! I'm sharing this example to illustrate the types of challenges that all women face, both intentionally and unintentionally. During my MBA studies, we were working as a group of five on a high-stress, high-profile team project. The overall execution of our project was successful, though not without its challenges.

There was deliberate ambiguity surrounding the project, which impaired team dynamics. At one point of the project, my teammate Mitch (name changed) yelled at me, and I yelled back. In retrospect, and felt even at the time this was not one of my finer moments! I set an intention to learn from the experience and repair the relationship and invited Mitch on a walk. I hoped to work through the problems that were plaguing the team. The talk was staged and set up as being amicable, and I was focused on finding a tangible outcome—a positive result.

Within the first three minutes, Mitch informed me that, "You need to recognize that as a woman, you are a minority in the business world."

I caught my breath and braced myself for the unexpected direction the conversation was taking. While I was not surprised that gender played a role in the challenges I felt while working in my group, I did not expect such a grandiose assertion so soon into the discussion, from a caring, thoughtful, hard-working peer, no less.

Mitch continued, "...so you need to change your behavior. If you see a hole in the project or a flaw in my logic, you can't just come out and say it. Instead, you need to make delicate recommendations until I get there on my own, and try to massage my ego, above all else."

That immediately shot me to the pinnacle of frustration. I paused before responding to Mitch. Before business school, my ability to recognize problems and find solutions was always seen as a positive strength. I detached emotion and made a rapid assessment: Mitch had the purest intentions to help me succeed. While a counter argument was that the actual problem lay in his expectations and gender stereotypes; I also realized that his decision to make this proclamation—in the year 2013—required a hefty lack of self-awareness. I felt ill-prepared for such a bold statement. Sadly, I found his announcement to be shocking, yet not actually surprising.

Before this, I had begun working with professors to learn the communication tools used by successful businesswomen, which had led to a period of immense personal and professional growth. It opened my eyes to the ways in which gender influences even the most basic of interactions

"Mitch, I want you to know that any time I offer a view counter to yours, my intent is to create stronger results for our team" he looked at me and seemed to be listening. "Please realize that a difference in opinion has nothing to do with you personally, but is instead aimed at achieving the best possible results. Can you reframe this in your approach?"

He nodded, "Yeah, I can do that."

The conversation left me exasperated. I had the opportunity to ask Sheryl Sandberg about this event during her *Lean In* book tour, and while she was sympathetic, her response roughly amounted to, "We as women have a steeper hill to climb, and there is simply more that we need to do."

The challenge then becomes: You can't fix a problem that you don't know exists. I sought counsel from a trusted professor and began to learn the laundry list of ways that I, similar to many women, had inadvertently held myself back: Smiling while giving feedback (contrary to my prior beliefs, a smile does not always communicate teamwork and optimism); Raising voices at the end of sentences; Acting less assertive in coed settings than in a group of women in order to keep my likability high.

As I uncovered my blind spots, my interest in improving my communication techniques only grew. I led workshops to help my colleagues avoid common communication pitfalls. In acting in ways that communicated confidence, I found that I became more confident, too.

This looped back to my experience studying in Italy. I think many Americans abroad go through a phase of trying to blend in with the locals as if altering behavior or dress will fast-track a feeling of acceptance. Now, this was easy for my friends with Italian heritage, but I have no Mediterranean lineage, and tricking the locals into thinking that I, too, was local, was simply not an option. I could not pretend to be someone or something I'm not. How exhausting it must be to maintain a façade or guess what other people may be thinking to adjust your own actions! Realizing that blending in was both fruitless and unnecessary helped me *own* who I was. This empowered me to find amazing friends and opened doors to better daily interactions. I didn't know it then, but the decision to be just me has also served me well in business and of course, in every element of my life.

This experience fast-tracked a turning point in my life. Knowing my most authentic self—who I am, and who I'm not—allows me to act from a centered and guided place of inner power. This makes decisions easier, of course, and helps me better identify opportunities that are suitable for both personal and professional growth. It also allows me to focus on my top priorities instead of worrying that I'm achieving somebody else's set of concerns.

Instead of emphasizing the potential risk of a given situation, I envision additional opportunities or solutions. When moving toward goals that are meaningful to me, I, therefore, feel empowered to do so with confidence.

I had a history of leadership roles throughout my life but never considered myself to be a businesswoman. I never imagined that the same skills that enabled me to successfully lead as Student Body President or to manage, direct and emcee 500+ person events are, essentially, business skills: Listening, problem-solving, analyzing, acting, creating. I am creative, curious, and compassionate, and viewed myself and business to be fundamentally opposed. How glad I am to have evolved on this point of view! Throughout my life, I've had many thoughts of, 'Someone should do this!' or, 'When will someone invent that?' Realizing my creative and tangible skills had a home in the field of entrepreneurship helped me to understand that I had the power to implement changes and to become my version of 'that someone.'

When I considered my experience of becoming fluent in Italian, I discovered parallel thoughts that questioned what differentiated my experience from that which many English learners in America face. I daydreamed about new possibilities and sky-high aspirations that could empower millions of people around the world. Teaching English in Italy had allowed me to learn fundamentals of English acquisition, and I came to understand that our language is quite simple in its initial stages of learning. This knowledge only furthered my belief that resources available to low-income immigrants were supremely ill-suited to their needs.

While completing my MBA, I learned how to refine the opportunity, size the market, and find a business model that was not only scalable but also sustainable. The realization that my idea did not simply feel good, but also discovering a viable path to success was equal parts surprising, exhilarating, and daunting. While eager to develop this venture to begin providing a voice to millions of people around the world, I was also aware of my lack of corporate experience and sought an internship that would help fill the gaps in my professional development.

I worked at TripAdvisor throughout business school and shortly after graduation. My first role was in a unique niche of the company that operated more like a startup than a corporation. Serendipitously, my Italian skills made me a prime candidate for this role. I was part of a team that created a program from the ground up, backed by the many resources of the company. I was incredibly fortunate to work for an inspiring and talented female boss while also learning about business relationships in the hotel industry. I also learned of the challenges presented in managing a multilingual workforce.

I subsequently worked in multiple departments at TripAdvisor until I felt confident to pursue my own venture full-time. Concurrently, I participated in the Babson WIN Lab in my off-hours, an application-based incubator program for high-potential female entrepreneurs. I reached a tipping point while there and realized that my lack of time was the primary factor limiting the progress of my company. Market research and customer interviews left me no doubt that an opportunity was waiting just around the corner, and taking the leap to devoting myself full-time to my business was incredibly exciting!

In under four months, my far-away vision on the horizon had turned into specific goals and outcomes, and we were launching a pilot test with the Four Seasons Hotel in Miami. My company, Entrada, connects the dots between the resources needed to develop English proficiency and the learning opportunities available to low-income immigrants.

In the very early stages of my business, I set my sights on one partnership which could serve as an entrance into my initial target market. Thinking, 'An email can't hurt!' I found the appropriate corporate contact on LinkedIn, wrote a brief introduction and requested a meeting. Here's an excerpt from what I said in my email: "Next week, I have a meeting with a potential client in your city, and I hope that you would be available to discuss these possibilities. I will be there from the 2nd through the 4th of March and hope that we could meet, ideally on Tuesday the 3rd. The meeting will take no more than 30 minutes. If time in this window is not feasible, I would be happy to arrange a meeting at your convenience."

He replied on the same day, and I refreshed my inbox multiple times to make sure that his response was there. Did I imagine it? Was this happening? Opening my email account again, there his email remained, sitting politely on the top line of my inbox.

By this point, I had proof of concept and very little else and definitely did not have a client meeting in his city. I do not know what compelled him to say yes, but he did!

To prepare, I had countless meetings with mentors, did a lot of yoga and meditation, and practiced many an inner dialogue in the weeks leading up to the main event. I prepared and rehearsed a grand introduction, aiming to build credibility and weave together a compelling story of how we could work together to enable change that was good for both business and society.

When the day came, and we met, I did power poses in the bathroom and took deep breaths to stop my voice from shaking. I started as rehearsed by introducing both myself and my company. About four sentences in, I realized my approach and preparation weren't what this guy was looking for, and he was already showing signs of disinterest. I tossed it all out the window, cut to the chase and made my ask: "Do you have plans now or in the future to address the low-income immigrant population?"

He sat up a bit, "No. We don't," he admitted.

"In that case, would you be interested in working with us?"

He almost smiled, "Yes, I think we would."

Within ten minutes that first meeting was over, and I was one step closer to my business goal. I left with a handshake and a promise that he would follow up within the next two weeks.

Entrada enables low-income immigrants to integrate into American culture, primarily by learning English as they work, using scientifically developed audio software and support materials. High-potential employees clip our audio player to their uniforms and engage with their English lessons as they work: One lesson per day. Our Learner Engagement Program provides learning prompts and support in a transportable, accessible, and fun manner.

Our holistic approach develops critical thinking skills, psychological confidence and more. In 100 lessons, learners can become fully conversational in English. By investing in staff education, employers benefit from improved operations and customer service. Moreover, recruitment and retention are proven to increase with bolstered employee engagement, not to mention the positive goodwill garnered by enabling staff to learn English. Entrada creates upward mobility for low-income immigrants, improves the public perception of businesses, and is a for-profit company.

* * *

I have learned many tricks along the way while starting and building my business. Here are the most important ones.

Entrepreneurs are faced with the decision to take on a partner or to be a sole founder. Research shows that ventures that begin with a team of founders are more likely to succeed, and I felt immense pressure to find a co-founder. While I found one immediately, I soon realized that I was more effective on my own. We have since parted ways, a very common experience that is rarely discussed in academic settings. This was possible, in part, due to a talented group of entrepreneurs who provided support when I needed it most. However, if you are looking for a co-founder, here are some tips for vetting prospective partners or co-founders:

- As is necessary for every other stage of your business: don't forget to check your assumptions! Have frank conversations about time and resources. Remain optimistic without being idealistic.
- Look for complimentary skill sets to your own.
- Have frank discussions about time and financial availability.
- Set clear expectations for founding members, with clearly outlined roles and requirements.
- Don't shy away from the difficult conversations, and don't be so attached to finding a solution that you impede the overall success of your company.

My top three pieces of advice for those interested in starting their own business are taken from Entrada's Core Values:

1. Identify the root of the problem, and work to solve it. You will be spending massive amounts of time and energy building your company. Make sure that it's a cause about which you are passionate.
2. Approach daunting tasks one step at a time. Often ideas are big and intimidating, but once you dive in, you realize that everything is manageable and within reach—provided you are persistent and keep your eye on your ultimate goal.
3. Ask for help when needed. Nobody can do it alone. Help can be found from mentors, friends, family, customers, clients... everyone, really! In fact, our Learner Engagement Program was crafted with guidance from a housekeeper at the Four Seasons who participated in our pilot test. In Cuba, she worked as a workplace psychologist and made our program even stronger. Don't expect people to offer blindly, you must ask for help to receive it.

This advice is what guides me every day. Entrada exists to empower individuals around the world to communicate. Currently, we offer the program in Spanish only and are working with housekeepers and cleaners. In the future, we hope to expand to more languages and to reach more professions. Our dream is to help with refugee assistance around the world, creating a more compassionate, communicative society in the process. Paso a paso!

To me, success is as simple as being happy. My experiences have taught me that for me to be truly happy – not merely content – I need to be challenged in ways that contribute to my personal growth. I require new situations to test, shape and strengthen the strong ethics to which I strive to adhere. I must also be working toward something that will prove transformational for myself or for others. Further, I must be surrounded by a strong group of intelligent and passionate peers. When these aspects of my life are fulfilled, I produce my best work and find happiness in the truest sense of the word. While happiness is not a static state, and success is never permanent, my outlook empowers me to feel both happy and successful more often than not!

About Erin Janklow

Erin Janklow is a firm believer that communication is key to success. She is committed to creating tools that enable others to succeed. She spent her early 20s in Italy, where she developed and maintained fluency in Italian through cultural and educational immersion. While living in Rome, she taught English as a Second Language to students of all ages, developing and perfecting techniques to enable learners to progress in their studies at a rapid yet sustainable pace.

Fluent in Italian and advanced in Spanish, Erin holds an MBA in Social Entrepreneurship from the F.W. Olin Graduate School of Business at Babson College, a B.A. from Northwestern University, and was selected as a member of the Babson WIN Lab. At Babson, she learned about social enterprise and discovered a profitable and scalable model to empower individuals around the world to communicate. She worked at TripAdvisor throughout business school and shortly afterward before leaving to start Entrada.

Entrada
WWW.ENTRADAESL.COM

Entrada is a social enterprise with an innovative solution to the growing challenge of managing a multilingual workforce. Most roles available to limited English speakers are physically difficult and follow a daily routine. Enabling low-income immigrants to integrate into American culture, primarily by learning English as they work, provide intellectual engagement and keeps productivity high. Pilot tests confirm that learners can maintain productivity in their daily tasks while simultaneously developing proficiency in the English language using their methodology. Entrada is also developing a Talk Back Methodology to allow learners to develop all skills needed to engage in English beyond the classroom. This holistic approach to learning develops critical thinking skills, psychological confidence and more.

Tearing Down to Rebuild and Restart Can Lead to Success

ERICKA MICHELLE LASSAIR

"If you work hard at your passion... you will see that your dreams are not the only dreams that can come true."
—ERICKA MICHELLE LASSAIR

The Master of Ceremony stepped up to the microphone to announce the winner of the $10,000 pitch competition. I felt flushed, hot, and my legs began to shake uncontrollably. This contest was beyond important to me. It was the one thing I thought could save me.

I was in a deep, dark, hole since closing my restaurant. I was flat broke, living with my parents and hiding my car to prevent it from getting repossessed (which was painfully ironic because, in my pre-restaurant career in the financial industry, I used to send accounts out to be repossessed). For the first time in my life, I was depressed and could not shake it. I had no hope for the future and thought I might have to file bankruptcy, which would prevent me from getting a loan for years. And I was embarrassed to get a regular job because I felt like a complete failure and disappointment.

So, this moment meant everything to me. During the competition period, I had made myself attend the last few pitch preparations and classes. I refused to practice my pitch in front of my competitors. The day of the final pitch, I wore the unique chef jacket dress I had designed and my lucky four-inch red heels. Despite the pressure and worry, something inside told me I could win. I knew that if I did, the depression would go away because then there was optimism for my future.

At the competition, I was first out of five to deliver my five-minute pitch with its supporting PowerPoint presentation. I grabbed all the judges' attention by describing my delicious food as pictures of it displayed in the background. I was confident, poised, and passionate. I wanted everyone to feel that I deserved this win! Afterward, I was smiling and happy, knowing I had done a good job. Sitting in the audience I watched my competitors, in support of them, because even though I wanted—needed to—win, I had built great relationships and respected each of them.

Literally, on the edge of my seat, legs twitching, I waited for the winner to be announced. I was close enough to hear my name from the emcee's lips as it passed through the microphone and came out of the speakers around the room with just a hint of echo. Tears—like I had never cried before—flowed so heavily I could barely give a Thank You speech. As I tried to form the words, inside my head, I shouted, 'I WON! I ACTUALLY WON!'

I've never won anything in my life and stayed on that winning high for a few days. Then the reality, that it was not going to be the solution to my problems, set in. Despite the $10,000 I had won, having poor credit ruined my hopes of getting the additional funding—a loan—to execute my business plan. That realization kicked me right back into that deep dark hole.

* * *

I grew up in a big family in New Orleans where we love to celebrate holidays, mostly because food is involved. Mardi Gras was the biggest because my grandmother lived uptown on the route of all the parades so everyone would come to her home. Always full of delicious meals, her house was where all my cousins and I went to play together.

Growing up, I learned how to cook and loved it. I was soon adding my own contributions to our family dinners. Christmas was the most important because we celebrated my grandmother's birthday on Christmas Eve by going to mass, having homemade egg nog, and sharing gifts. We all loved my grandmother, and I have always idolized her because she worked extremely hard, but still had a ton of fun. One thing she never showed was her difficulties as she supported her family of eight kids after my grandfather passed away from lung cancer.

That willingness to work hard day in and day out, never complaining or losing a love for life, was passed on to my mom. I never knew how much she struggled to support me until I was a teenager and wanted more things. But my mom and Nanny (godmother) made me feel that shopping at the thrift store was like going to a designer boutique. And I would be excited to get clothes no one else would be wearing. I shake my head and laugh at that now!

My mom had a great support system, and I was always loved and well taken care of by family members and her close friends. She had divorced my biological father when I was a baby, and he was in jail. She chose to raise me on her own with the support of his mother and sister, yet gave him the option to help her if he wanted to. She always sent me to visit him. But being an independent soul, I decided early in life a relationship with a drunk that is in and out of jail with no steady income, even if he was my father, wasn't what I wanted. He made me see that having toxic people in my life is not good for my—or anyone's for that matter—happiness and peace of mind.

While mom laid down the rules in my life, my grandmother made an impact on me more by just watching her. I'm an observer by nature, and my grandmother was a quick mover. On some days after classes, my mom and I would help her clean the school where she was the head janitor. When there were school events, we helped her set up decorations, chafers, and food. At night, I would watch her get dolled up for Bingo, club meetings or whatever occasion she was going out for. I was fascinated by how hard she worked during the day, then would come home and put on makeup, heels, and a nice dress to enjoy her evening out. I asked her why she put powder on her face before she applied her makeup and she replied, "So my face doesn't get oily." Then I would ask,

"Grandma, how can you wear heels after working hard and being on your feet all day?" And she would reply, "Because I love heels and they keep the arch in my feet from hurting." Her answers always affirmed that she was in control of her life. She knew what she wanted and needed to do.

Riding in the car with my grandmother, whether it was going two blocks or 20 miles, was always an adventure. She drove as she walked—FAST! Grandma loved her city of New Orleans and loved to share its history and her experience working in certain mansions for parties and special events. One time we were in the car, and she was so involved in telling her story—pointing out the place and getting into the details—she almost hit someone. It was funny since she didn't, but from that day on grandma was more cautious and slowed down her speedy driving. She learned and moved on.

One thing she told me that I still live my life by is that if you work hard, enjoy your life while you can. I admired a lot in my grandmother, but to see her travel all over the world really had an effect. It gave me the fearlessness to start traveling at a young age. And just from watching her, I learned that to enjoy life you must be engaged in it.

In 2001, I graduated from Southern University in Baton Rouge, Louisiana with a B.S. degree in Business Marketing. From there, I moved to Dallas,

Texas and worked in finance for six years. It was at that job when I realized that people really loved my cooking. When we had company potluck meals, every dish I made would be the first one finished with a request for more at the next one. Then I got requests from people interested in buying the dishes I had prepared or offers to pay me to make someone else's potluck dish. When cooking competitions came around, I won them all. Friends began encouraging me to consider cooking professionally and to possibly open a restaurant. I thought the idea was too risky and that I wasn't skilled enough to take on that large of a task.

Then my finance job changed from a position where I traveled and had the freedom to make my schedule—something I enjoyed a great deal—back to an office and a desk job, which I did not like. That's when it hit me that I was not happy and something was missing in my life. I quit my job and moved back home with no idea how I was going to start over but determined to find a way. After months of not working, I finally landed a job a Saks Fifth Avenue. I knew my time there was limited and needed to figure out if I was going to culinary school and where I would go.

In 2008, I was accepted into culinary school but had to get another job, an apprenticeship at Commander's Palace a five-star restaurant. This was a sad day for me because it only paid $8 an hour, and I had to pay for school. Even with two jobs, I couldn't afford to go to school and rent an apartment, too. That meant I was going to have to live at my parent's house for longer than I had planned.

One day, as I transitioned from finishing culinary school, auditioning for the Next Food Network Star, and working at Saks Fifth Avenue, a craving hit me. I wanted a hot dog but not just a plain one. I had been thinking about opening a restaurant with a creative concept but had not come up with anything distinctive. That craving was my light bulb moment of inspiration. I started writing ideas down and thinking of different ways to prepare hot dogs. Then it hit me, make them reflect the flavor of my hometown, New Orleans! I took a traditional American food and paired it with my love of New Orleans food. The name Diva Dawg came easily to me because a great group of friends always called me Diva and since it was a different kind of hot dog, I spelled dog, D A W G.

That was the concept I embraced and ran with. I worked to develop and refine it and then using what resources I had, found a location I liked and worked to open my own restaurant. It was an exciting—and scary—time of my life.

One thing about me is I never test my ideas, and rarely taste my food before I serve it. It's a weird superstition developed after noticing I did it unknowingly after years of cooking. Before the grand opening of Diva Dawg, my friends and family asked me tons of times if I was going to let them try my dawgs before I sold and served them to the public. I said no and got some curious looks, but I was determined to stick with what had worked for me in the past. My friends and family were all scared on the day of opening, but I saw everything in my dreams before it happened. I knew the opening would be great. And it was. People were hesitant to try this different concept but loved it once they did. All my original recipes have been launched the same way since day one.

After my first three months in business, everything was great. I thought it could only go up from there, but then it didn't.

The location I loved so much proved to be a poor choice, finding reliable employees was hard, and my bills were more than I budgeted. I struggled for months not paying myself and could only pay my employees half their pay on paydays and had to scramble to get them caught up later. That became a seemingly endless cycle. Checks regularly bounced, I was consistently three months behind on rent, my car was out for repossession, so I had to hide it at the dealership where my brother worked. Finally, after getting a small advance loan to try to catch up on bills, I decided to give up on my dream and closed the restaurant the week of Thanksgiving. It was a year and three months after opening its doors.

For months, I had struggled on the inside but always managed to smile in public. Then as my world was falling in around me, I hid from everyone and then even from myself. I went into a depression so deep it seemed I would never be able to climb out. Was I not as strong as I thought I was? Why was I crying all the time and why did I have thoughts of ending my life, why? I could not shake the feeling. Nothing or no one could help me, I thought. Until I realized, I was in a competition that could help me restart my business. That pulled me out enough to make the decision I needed to make, to close my restaurant. And to set my heart on winning that competition. That would turn things around for me!

I started the competition in September, and it continued until March with classes and pitch practice sessions. Working from the end of my fixed location restaurant, I began to focus on reorganizing my business. A clear vision was needed to see where it could go. That focus and determination helped me to win the $10k pitch competition and give Diva Dawg a new start as a food truck and catering operation. But how was I going to get someone to finance me and provide the rest of the money needed? All the bad credit I had accrued from trying to save the restaurant, made it difficult to fund a re-launch.

I consulted with my cousin Andre as I always did on financial matters. Seeking a savior for the restaurant during its last few months of operation I had asked him a few times to partner with me. He didn't say yes or no, but his hesitancy told me exactly what he thought of the restaurant's prospects. I thought I would get the same response when I asked him to partner with me on the food truck, hoping to make Diva Dawg a family business. Fortunately, when I asked him this time, it was a yes!

A food truck concept—with lower overhead costs—made it a more acceptable risk for Andre. He was right to not commit to helping me save the restaurant. But his quick agreement about the food truck made me uneasy, and I constantly asked him "Are you sure?" The question I asked myself, too was 'Am I sure I can do this again, and succeed this time?' It constantly ran through my mind since I now had my cousin to consider. I didn't want him to experience failure as I had. But over time his passion for Diva Dawg eased that fear. His great credit allowed us to get financing for the truck in August 2014 and we hit the ground running. We passed all the inspections, found a commissary kitchen to supply us ingredients and prep space and opened October 2014, just in time for National Chili Month.

And each year has gotten better since!

It took me a while to get over the closing of my restaurant and to find myself. But that hardship taught me a lot and not just about the right and wrong things to do or not do in business. I now trust myself more and never second guess my gut feeling or inner voice. I am grateful for all the opportunities in life that I get and don't regret those I don't get.

I know that what is meant for me in my life—the good things—will last if I continue to work hard and focus on what I'm passionate about. I also know that continuing to educate myself and others around me will get us all further in life. Being an inspiration to others has changed my perception of my dream. I see now that the dream is no longer just mine, but it is everyone's who supports and is inspired by it. And in some way, I can help them find and focus on their own goals. The moves I make in my life now are to show them to be fearless and that you can accomplish your objectives with hard work, dedication and most of all passion. I tell others to embrace, celebrate and expect failure because it will make them stronger. Be passionate about the business you want to start, and only take advice from those experienced in that field or who have had a business before.

Don't become paralyzed by questioning why a business idea did not work out. At some point—sooner rather than later—you must move on and learn from it. And always have faith that the finest is yet to come. Ironically, three years after I moved out of the brick and mortar on Magazine Street, Diva Dawg opened in a local market called Roux Carre the week of

Thanksgiving in November 2016. And even with that good news, I know more is ahead for me.

Success to me is happiness. When I started my journey, I was running away from unhappiness. Though financially secure, I was always away from family, friends and bored with the everyday routine of my job. I knew I had to make a break to find myself even if it meant starting over making $8 hour, living with my parents and giving up my free car. The struggle of starting over proved to be the most successful decision I've ever made. It is the reason I found my happiness.

ABOUT ERICKA MICHELLE LASSAIR

Ericka Michelle Lassair a.k.a 'Chef Diva' is a New Orleans native, the owner, and chef of Diva Dawg Food Truck. After graduating from Southern University in Baton Rouge, Louisiana with a degree in marketing, she worked in finance in Dallas.

Six years later, following Hurricane Katrina, she decided it was time to move home and help rebuild her city. She enrolled in culinary school at Delgado and worked at the historic five-star restaurant Commander's Palace before opening her restaurant, Diva Dawg, in 2012.

Ericka has appeared on Destination America's *Last Call Food Brawl*, as well as several local news and radio programs. Also, she is the 2014 winner of the Urban League of Greater New Orleans WIB Challenge and the 2015 Capital One Business Plan Pitch winner.

She is currently a Tory Burch Foundation 2016 Fellow and was featured in the January 2017 issue of Vogue magazine with Tory Burch. In July 2017, watch for her and the Diva Dawg Truck appearance in the movie, *Girl Trip*.

Diva Dawg
WWW.DIVADAWG.COM

Diva Dawg, a gourmet hot dog joint, launched in September 2012 on Magazine Street in New Orleans and two years later began rolling as a food truck.

The brand's signature 'Diva Dawg,' is an all-beef hot dawg paired with a sweet and savory bun and Creole toppings. Other offerings include the Red Bean Chili Dawg topped with fried chicken (featured as one of CondéNast Traveler's *Outrageous Hot Dogs in the United States*), homemade Crawfish Etouffee Fries, Crabmeat Grill Cheesy and Praline Candy Shake.

In 2015, BET spotlighted Diva Dawg as one of its top ten black-owned businesses to visit in New Orleans while Eater New Orleans recently named the Diva Dawg Truck 'one of the hottest food trucks in New Orleans.' Diva Dawg can be found at 2000 Oretha Castle Haley Blvd in the Roux Carre food market. It's not a hot dog... it's a Diva Dawg!

A Debilitating Disease Leads to a Healthy New Business

IRINA SKOERIES

"At any given moment, you have the power to say: this is not how the story is going to end."

—ANONYMOUS

"You'll never be able to run again in your life."

I couldn't quite hear what the rheumatologist mumbled as he studied my medical charts. What I thought he had said shocked me. "Excuse me, what did you say?"

He looked up at me, "You're not going to be able to run." He saw the look that had already formed on my face, "But we should be able to manage your symptoms with medication."

The rest of the conversation was not much better. Four weeks before this grave news I had gone to bed as a seemingly very fit, healthy young mother. The next morning, I woke with a hand so inflamed and painful that I couldn't touch it or even try to bend my fingers. Within two weeks, that inflammation and pain had spread throughout my body (feet, shoulder, neck, left arm). I couldn't walk or use my right hand, lift my left arm or turn my head. Crippled by immense pain, I was sent from doctor to doctor, specialist to specialist and finally was diagnosed with a supposedly incurable autoimmune disease, Rheumatoid Arthritis.

All the doctors could tell me was to expect that—maybe—I would be able to semi-function with daily doses of powerful drugs. But I had tried the prescribed medication, and there was hardly any change.

The constant hurt was killing me. Standing in my kitchen one morning I figuratively stomped my foot (I couldn't in real life because of the pain). I did not want drugs to 'manage' my symptoms. I wanted to live and enjoy a healthy body and lifestyle!

Something happened as I faced what all the doctors were telling me, a life of diminishing quality. I was not going to accept what they said would be my fate. I was 35 years old and had two young children. Who would take care of them if my condition worsened, which was likely, and I was unable to do work of any kind? As a single mother, it scared me more than how I felt about myself, my own health and future. What would happen to my children?

At that moment, all the thoughts tumbling around in my head stopped. Everything became very clear. I vowed that it—my condition—would not dictate the rest of my life. I swore that I would find a way, some treatment, that would help me. And not by covering up my symptoms with hardcore drugs. Committed to finding something that would work where the drugs hadn't, I felt that healing myself would come through learning how to feed myself right.

I have always been a very health conscious person. An ecological agriculture major in college, I had followed a mostly gluten free and organic diet and was aware of the healing power of food. I had even reversed my oldest son's dental decay through diet change. However, reprogramming my body to recover from the massive, systemic, inflammation that was shutting down more of my body every day required examining every single choice I made for what entered my body and mind.

Luckily, I could connect with the very accomplished Ann Boroch, a naturopathic doctor, who helped me come to grips with what I needed to do to become symptom-free from my autoimmune disease. Ann gave me a long to-do list which included food that would help my body reprogram itself so my immune system would stop attacking healthy tissues and joints. Armed and determined, I set out to restore my health. It became the focus of my self-treatment: low glycemic, anti-inflammatory ingredients prepared in delicious dishes and meals. I did with food what drugs couldn't! Food was and is my most important medicine to combat my disease. That along with intention and willpower healed my body and soul.

I guess it is not a surprise that food and nature would be a savior in my life. I grew up in Germany in a small town. My family comes from the Alsace region, and there was always a lot of delicious food, cooking, art, and nature around me. The things that sustain and nurture your soul. I had planned to become a graphic designer, but after I spent a summer working with at-risk youth on a small island on the west coast of Scotland, I decided to pursue a degree in ecological agriculture. I came to America, studied in California, where I've worked in school gardens and as an environmental educator, and have been here in Santa Barbara ever since.

One of the primary reasons I pursued going to college in the United States was because I had fallen in love with an American man while working in Scotland. I wanted to continue my studies, and since he didn't want to move to Germany, I decided to go to California. We then chose to get married. I finished my studies, started working and became pregnant with my first son. Six years later, the same year my husband and I divorced, I gave birth to my second son. After I had my first child, I became the wine manager at a boutique hotel and restaurant and worked in that industry for six years. I was always curious to learn from the chefs in the kitchen and copied what they were doing in my own kitchen, though I never wished to become a chef myself.

With having an American ex-husband and father who wanted to see his children as much as I did, there was no option for me to move back to Germany. Unless I wanted my kids traveling back and forth on intercontinental flights with long stretches of time of being away from the other parent. That financial and emotional burden would have been too hard for our family. But often when so ill, I wished I could have moved back to Germany. Its health care system would have paid a lot of my medical bills, supported me in my healing process and with financial aid and childcare.

If I hadn't gotten sick my life would be very different today (I would probably still be working as a fine-dining and wine manager). I became a different person because of my experience pushing through and recovering from all the pain and that terrible feeling of potentially dying relatively young. Now, I wonder sometimes if my recovery is like a butterfly when they come into this world, or a phoenix rising from ashes. I had endured not just pain, but that everything had changed in me, who I was... my body, and with that much of my identity. Accepting that it was better to not move—or do so as little as possible—just to avoid the stabbing agony in my joints affected everything in my life. Movement was like pushing through a thick swamp of glue that hadn't quite set into a solid. The pain slowed and hindered me, not letting me move freely as I used to and remembered so vividly in my mind. But even with bone and tissue screaming, I managed to get moving. If I hadn't, I would not have discovered what would save me.

It was not easy, but worth it! Through the suffering and desperation, the doubt, worries, and tears, I gained something I would never have otherwise: my mission in life. Thank goodness for that rheumatologist in Montecito telling me I would never be healthy again because there is one thing that I have seen now, in myself as a result. If someone tells me I can't do something and that 'something' is important to me, a force awakens in me that cries out in German: "DOCH," which means YES, I CAN, and I will show you! So, with the doctor's "No," he gave me a reason to find the strength to say 'YES, I WILL.'

In the process of recovering from my body shutting down and then rebooting it, I lost my well-paying job and was left with almost zero income. I was blessed with short-term help from my parents to pay my bills (I don't receive any financial support from my ex-husband). However, I had to start making money soon and was faced with the choice to go back to what I did before—my old server job—or to risk the unknown. I knew I had to share what had cured me but had no idea if it would be a way I could make a living to support my family.

That a human's real wealth is his or her health was something I had learned through bitter and painful experience. And there were others out there suffering and in pain. As I discovered what foods worked best in my own healing, I found that there is close to none of it readily available in our Western world. I began to see it as my responsibility to change that, in my lifetime, and provide as many people as possible with the prepared foods that help heal and create peace in the body.

Being sick and then recovering through a means I developed for myself, gave me the courage to listen to that voice inside no matter how scary the unknown was. I had to start cooking for people—preparing for them the very things that had helped make me healthier—and figure out how to make money doing it. Starting my business didn't seem like a choice to me. I had to do it.

I built a website and made business cards and called myself a private chef specializing in an anti-inflammatory cuisine. I did not have any formal training and was strictly self-taught. My boldness wasn't because I had no doubts... I was unsure about what I was doing and the outcome, but took a risk and did what had to be done. I had to define myself and then prove to others I could do for them what I had done for myself.

In the process of building my website, I ran into some questions that required the advice of someone with more experience in the business world. I've learned you must be brave enough to go after what you want and need in life. And though I was nervous I reached out to someone in Santa Barbara who was a friend of a friend. I didn't know too much about him or his business, but I knew from bits and pieces of conversations that he could probably give me the advice I needed. So, I wrote him a Facebook message, asking him for a brief meeting if he would be willing to help me with the questions I had. I have to laugh about my brashness here because I was absolutely unaware that I had just contacted the head of one of the most successful financial investment and wealth management companies in Santa Barbara. I boldly asked him to make time in his busy schedule to see me!

The beautiful thing is that this man, Seth Streeter, CEO of Mission Wealth, made the time that week to see me. You should have seen me walking into his posh office and thinking: 'Wow! Who did I ask to make time for me?!' But then I gathered my composure quickly because after what I'd gone through, nothing daunted me anymore. We had a fantastic very productive and helpful meeting (1.5 hours instead of the 15 min. I asked for), and it was the beginning of an amazing friendship. To thank him for his time I delivered some food to him, and he told me afterward: "If all your food tastes like that, you are going to make millions of dollars."

Seth is the reason why I created one of my products, GOGO Balls because I wanted to give him a much healthier alternative to the energy bars he was eating. It became clear to me that the rest of the world needs them, too!

After my website was up, I started to cook for a couple of people I connected with through friends and health practitioners that recommended me. Then one day I get a phone call.

"I'm looking for a private chef," a woman's voice started talking as soon as I picked up the phone. "I live in Montecito and have to tell you I like to surround myself with happy people."

"That sounds wonderful," I told her. "I also aim to surround myself with as much happiness as possible."

"My husband and I are leaving for Mexico and will be there a while, but I wanted to give you a call before we go." She gave me her name. "I'll call you when we get back."

I said, "That's great, I look forward to hearing from you."

Weeks passed, and I heard nothing from her. Then when I checked on Craigslist for private chef openings, there was a listing in Montecito for a private chef, and I sent in my information. A personal assistant called me to set up an interview and then afterward I would be required to do a cooking demo at the client's estate.

The Mister and the Lady of the house were gone at that time, but they had narrowed down the 300 applications they got for the job opening to three, one of them being me. So, I came and cooked for the personal assistant and other house staff. At one point, as we were standing in the biggest pantry I have ever seen, the personal assistant said to me: "The Lady of the house, Katia (not her real name) only likes this kind of drinking water…"

I said, "Katia! You don't mean Katia Edelheit?" That was the name of the women that had called me weeks ago. I recalled it because it was a very uncommon first and last name in America but very common in Germany.

The personal assistant looked and me and said, "Yes, Katia Edelheit, do you know her?"

I told her about Katia's phone call to me weeks before. So, there I was… chosen by this household to be interviewed twice, independently from each other.

After I passed the initial cooking test, I cooked for a week in rotation with the other applicant for the job, which resulted with me being offered the position. I feel like the luckiest private chef on Earth. I don't call my private chef work for Mr. and Mrs. Edelheit a cooking job; it is a paid internship. An internship for life, where I'm being advised by two of the most brilliant minds in the U.S.A.!

Through Mr. and Mrs. Edelheit I connected with Dr. Steven Gundry, who is not only their doctor but also Tony Robbins's. Dr. Gundry is a world-renowned cardiologist, heart surgeon, and medical researcher. For the last 15 years, he has focused on improving health, happiness, and longevity through a unique vision of human nutrition, which happens to encompass the exact food list that restored my body. I am honored to say that Dr. Gundry is featuring one of my company's products: Catalysts Cuisine's KickStarter Protocol, in his newest book, called *The Plant Paradox,* published by HarperCollins.

One of the best pieces of advice Mr. Edelheit ever gave me came out of this scenario: I had attempted to cook his favorite dish, pasta with clams and a white wine reduction sauce and was unaware I had overcooked the clams. As he was eating his meal, in his most beautiful breathtaking estate and having experienced the world's best foods many times in his life, he commented to me: "These clams are very chewy!" He paused for a bit, and I started thinking, 'Oh no!' Then he proceeded to say, "But the sauce is very good. Can I have a bit more of that sauce, please?" What he taught me in this conversation was that there are always choices in life: you can either focus on the overcooked, chewy clams or on the delicious sauce. The choice is yours.

After working for about half a year as a private chef, as the new year came around I decided to commit myself to 12 days of eating 100% by the food list I had developed for optimized health. Busy with my kids, I made them quick, easy, meals that looked beautiful. I decided to take pictures of each meal and post them on my social network. After a few days, I realized that I had created a program that could be replicated and offered affordably as a food cleanse for anybody who wanted it. I started offering it to my clients as a 3-Day food cleanse. The timing with New Years was right, and demand was high. I realized that to reach as many bellies as possible, I had to be more than a private chef and needed to start a meal delivery company that provides—priced affordably for everyone—the meals that restored my health. Through my work in

Montecito, I had met an amazing group of successful, brilliant entrepreneurs and game changers. With their encouragement and guidance, I decided to become an entrepreneur myself, in addition to being a private chef, to provide as many people as possible with this food. The foundation for my meal delivery company Catalyst Cuisine was laid.

I continued to meet people that inspired me. One day David Nygren, a private chef client of mine told me he had invited some special guests over for dinner. "Olivia Newton-John is one of them," he mentioned as he gave me the details on how many guests and when to plan for the dinner.

I replied, "That sounds fantastic. I really look forward to making food for you all!"

Now, I had no idea who Olivia Newton-John was... not a clue. I just assumed since she was his guest that she must be important, as all his guests were. After he had walked away, as I was standing there, I searched her name on my smartphone. 'Oh!' I told myself, 'she was in that movie *Grease*.' When the evening for that dinner came, I focused solely on making a delicious meal for them. I had not given any more thought about who his guests were and if they were celebrities or stars. I didn't see when they arrived. My focus was in the kitchen preparing dinner, which was then served by waiters and servers to the dinner guests.

The main dishes had been served and finished. Shortly after dessert, Mr. Nygren asked me to come out from the kitchen. He knew about my background and why I had become a chef and thought it might be interesting for his guests to hear it. "Irina," he said, "would you tell my guests a little bit about your story?"

So, I did and then afterward introduced myself individually to the people around the table. That's when I met Olivia, and there was something about her, I didn't know what at the time but felt that we had made a connection in some way. Later, I learned more about her and discovered she had survived a life-threatening illness—cancer—that had been diagnosed when she was a relatively young age. I think that was what we sensed between us as a common bond when we met. I also learned that Olivia's husband is actively involved in the Amazon, in research to develop medicines from natural products in the rain forest, introducing new drugs to the Western world. And that linked to my background in ecological agriculture, so we had lots to talk about that evening.

It was a very pleasant evening just getting to talk with the dinner guests and to meet Olivia. But I thought it unlikely I would ever see her again. I told my mother about meeting her, and she got excited, "I used to have her poster on my wall!" I discovered that my mom was (still is) a big Olivia Newton-John fan and I grew up as a little girl listening to Olivia's songs, unaware of who was singing them.

Three weeks later I got a phone call. I didn't recognize the incoming number on my cell phone but answered it, "Hello."

The person on the other end of the call said, "Hi" and then hesitated just a second before continuing, "This is Olivia Newton-John. I don't know if you remember me or not but you cooked me dinner not long ago."

And that started a friendship. I found out her mom and I have the same first name. Her mother was also born in Germany and came to the United States about the same age that I did. Olivia asked me to cook for some of her dinner parties, and I also cook for her on her birthday. She is such an angel to be around and holds so much energy inside her. I love to be around her and the people she surrounds herself with. I told her about that moment in my kitchen when I became determined and so focused on overcoming fear and choosing to find a way to heal. Olivia said she had that exact moment as well, on her journey to recover from cancer. And that's why she wrote a song called, *Not Gonna Give Into It*.

Right around the same time I connected with another of the most incredible human beings on Earth, Jeff Conroy, now my business partner. He oversaw the creation of a café in a hip new co-working office, The

Impact Hub, in Santa Barbara. I knew after I met him once, that we were meant to create something of magnitude together. Jeff has led our meal delivery company from being an I-deliver-in-paper-bags-with-hand-written-notes to a nationwide delivery company serving thousands of people. His connections to very successful business mentors like Paul Orfalea (founder of Kinko's) have helped shape the development of this company significantly. Jeff is one of the most giving people, and I am beyond thankful to build this business with him. We both share many things, one being that we both have freckles in our eyes' iris. I haven't met another person who has this in common with me. I believe we both come from the same part of the universe, maybe the freckle star!

The result of meeting Jeff? I got myself a commercial kitchen, kickass business partner and started delivering my food nationwide.

Juggling my time and energy to be present with my sons and running my business at the same time, is a challenge I haven't overcome yet, but I do permit myself to not be perfect and have become more forgiving. Over the next twelve months, I'll need that as we grow Catalyst Cuisine to a million-dollar business by collaborating with other organizations, doctors, funders, backers, and celebrities who fully understand the extent and power of what we call 'food.' It contains the code that runs our most valuable possession, our bodies.

Successful software companies would never write program code that ruins the computer systems that run on it. That doesn't make any sense. So why then do we regularly—and happily—allow our most valuable asset (our bodies) to be programmed with a destructive code (inflammatory foods)? And why is it so difficult to find prepared food, that provides the body with what is right for it, that is both delicious and affordable?

We need as many healthy, happy people with well-fueled brains to come up with genius solutions, real fast, to the myriad of problems our world faces. That means we need to run those brains on a healthy operating system. The kind that can be developed by eating food that is optimized for you and not just what most of the food industry produces right now (which doesn't accelerate healing to improve health, but pleases your taste buds).

I'll close with this. Recently I was invited by Olivia Newton-John to see her show in Las Vegas. She dedicated one of her songs that night to me, and as I sat in the audience, I started crying. I was so moved by her words and voice as she sang about grace and gratitude. This is exactly what the journey of starting and running my business makes me feel, a deep awe and appreciation for life. And it all started that day, in my kitchen, when I stood there and stomped my foot, not willing to accept what had happened to me and took things into my own hands.

Success to me means overreaching my personal goals by increasing, as much as possible, the well-being and happiness of the people around me and that I connect with, to make everyone's world better and healthier.

About Irina Skoeries

Irina, who was diagnosed two years ago with a crippling, supposedly lifelong disease, is a private chef and caterer in Montecito, California. She is the Founder of Catalyst Cuisine and healed herself by eating foods that follow a strict formula that is a naturally evolved blueprint to accelerate health and encompasses as many anti-inflammatory components as possible.

She is living proof of the power of this way of eating. Irina wants to inspire and help people to reap its benefits and provides an easy and affordable way for the world to have access to this food through her business.

Catalyst Cuisine
WWW.CATALYSTCUISINE.COM

Catalyst Cuisine transforms lives. They deliver ready to eat meals prepared according to a strict formula that encompasses as many anti-inflammatory components as possible. Their meals provide the body with a blueprint naturally evolved to accelerate health. With nationwide delivery, they offer the easiest way to optimize your health through healthy and delicious food. Recognized and recommended by many, including singer/actress Olivia Newton-John, Catalyst Cuisine is also endorsed by Dr. Steven R. Gundry, M.D. and will be featured in his new book published by HarperCollins.

Everything You Do, Every Step You Take, Is What Makes You Who You Are

MEREDITH SORENSEN

"Everything—even trash—tells a story."
—MEREDITH SORENSEN

When I look at world maps, I can draw long lines over the ground that I have covered with my own two feet. One thing I know: we are all connected by this Earth.

My early 20s were shaped by long walks. Five days after graduating college, I went to Maine and set out from the northernmost tip of the 2,168-mile footpath known as the Appalachian Trail. Four and a half months later I took my final step in Georgia. Then, after many hot, soapy showers and time with family, I packed for West Africa and joined the Peace Corps in the Ivory Coast. Just as I was settling into my quintessential small village with straw huts, among people who spoke an obscure dialect–Kulango–we were evacuated due to a coup. Weary, but determined to fulfill my two-year obligation, I restarted my service in Madagascar in an even smaller village. In a culmination of these formative life experiences, I completed an 8-month hike the length of Madagascar, and along the way taught farmers about compost.

Toward the end of my journey, I decided that in the U.S., I would not own a car and work in the recycling industry. Many years later as I write this chapter, those caveats still hold true. It was also in Madagascar where I realized what business I wanted to be in, but more on that later.

I grew up in New Jersey with a picturesque childhood of family, gardens, and adventures on the shore—with a Bruce Springsteen soundtrack in the background. I now muse that it was the many landfills next to the turnpike, and beaches closed due to trash washing up on the shore that inspired my fascination with waste management. Another motivator was respect for the soil. When I was a child, I remember my parents always had a little bucket next to them when they gardened. In their early years, they could only afford cheap dirt from the borough's compost dump. As they worked the soil, they picked out unwanted bits and tossed them in the bucket. One glorious fall afternoon stands out in my memory: I helped my father screen our backyard compost bin, and we cheered at each discovery of grubs and earthworms, the natural tractors of the soil. Scoop by scoop, year by year, they took out the bad (bits of glass and plastic) and added good (compost), yielding an award-winning landscape.

My launch into college almost stalled out and required patience and persistence. I fell in love with Wellesley College the moment I visited its stunning campus with elegant lampposts and a strong, skilled student body of badass women. I applied, and then got waitlisted. I wasn't quite 'in.' This setback made me even more aware of my determination to attend. So, I created a poster of all my pursuits and activities and returned to campus to make my case. After going through the photos, I made my pitch to the admissions staff, focusing on the woman in charge, "I know I might not be the best student in the world, but I'm a dynamic person and want to be here. I'll take a year off between high school and college if that's what's necessary to become a Wellesley woman. What do I need to do?"

She replied, "You just did it."

That day I learned a lesson about showing up and telling my story, demonstrating that I was willing to go after and work for what I wanted. I graduated with the class of 2001.

Persistence played a role in getting into Wellesley, but I acutely felt the inner workings of my 'determination muscle' develop afterward on the Appalachian Trail while learning two opposing, yet complementary lessons. A few hundred miles in, during a climb up a mountain, I wanted desperately to get off the trail and go home. My commitment to complete the path wavered. At the top of the mountain, as hot tears flowed down my face, I decided to give myself a little freedom and adopted the following strategy: whenever I felt like quitting, I would give myself three days. If something didn't happen in those three days that changed my mind, I would step off the trail and go home. With this mindset, my spirit felt released and set free.

An inverse life lesson came on the trail from one of the Earth's smallest creatures that I met in the middle of a blistering day. With hiking—well, with any extended physical activity—one must regularly hydrate and fuel your body. You need to take periodic breaks and rest. Nature, to me, is beautiful in all its varieties and manifestations, but it was hot, my legs ached, and the pack was so heavy that it was hard to appreciate the woods all around me. I stopped, sank to the ground just off the trail and reached into my backpack for a granola bar and water bottle. Plain, ambient-temperature water tastes delicious when you're parched. And the salty-sweet granola bar was tasty, just what I needed. Between sips of water and bites of granola bar, I took a few deep breaths.

Taking a break from the trail felt good, and I was gazing at the ground by my legs, zoning out, when a movement caught my eye. I leaned forward for a closer look. A crumb from my granola bar had fallen on the ground, and an ant was headed toward it. The crumb was easily twice the size of the ant, who was now circling it. The ant stopped, and I wondered whether it had considered the morsel of food too large to handle, and was deciding to move on. But it didn't. The ant stepped up to the crumb and then levered its body underneath the edge, just enough to push up higher and get a grip. Fascinated, I watched—having to get on my knees and reposition and follow—as the ant carried that crumb 20 feet to its hole. It seemed a heroic effort to me. I had squatted down as I watched the ant's last shifting and maneuvering of the crumb, then rocked back on my heels. Suddenly, my 2,000+ mile hike didn't seem like such a big deal. Sure, that's a long way, and my pack was large and heavy. But it's all relative. That ant did what I had just observed, day in and day out. It made me realize that all people are on their own path—their own trail—pushing their crumb along, hoping to feast with family and friends at the end of their journey.

Those two experiences on the trail, watching the ant move that giant crumb and embracing quitting as an option, had a far-reaching impact on me. We're all carrying our proverbial crumbs with a certain level of drive and determination. More importantly, I learned that when you give yourself the freedom to quit, you ironically gain power. One moment, I was on the edge of giving up and telling myself, 'I have to stick this out' from a weak and pleading vantage point. The next moment, by shifting the language and mindset to, 'I am choosing to stay here... to remain in this (whatever 'this' might be) for this much longer,' I moved into a position of power and self-determination.

I applied this same realization and approach to rough patches when working overseas. By giving myself that freedom to leave and the mandate to look for signs for three days, I became even stronger, and my experience became enriched. Instead of wallowing in the struggle, I focused on possibilities of positive experiences. Poised on the brink of quitting, I'd shift to staying three more days, and would inevitably come upon a beautiful view or have an encounter with a bright soul. I'd then feel so alive and grateful for the tremendous opportunity to be out in the world—really out there—on trails, in huts, with people from different cultures, tending crops, learning languages. And everything, the effort, the challenges (both physical and mental), became worthwhile.

I had just settled into my first Peace Corps village, the one in Cote d'Ivoire, when the other volunteers and I were evacuated due to civil unrest. Authorities relocated us to the neighboring country of Ghana to see if things would settle down. Would I see my village again? Would I return to the U.S.? I hated being in limbo but felt guilty. There I was, in a nice hotel surrounded by friends, a food buffet, swimming pools, and a ticket to anywhere in the world. Meanwhile, my Ivorian friends back in the village were stuck with a shaky government and their biggest uncertainty, the weather. If the coming season was bad, and the rains weren't plentiful to help grow the yams, they faced great hardship. And it was completely out of their control.

Whereas, I did have a measure of control over my future. In my gut, I knew that I wanted to get to the end of the Peace Corps trail, but I still had many steps to take. I had signed up for two years and had completed only nine months in a village.

The situation in Cote d'Ivoire was still iffy; I had no idea when we could go back there or even if we would. That became moot when an opportunity came up in the interim, and eighteen other volunteers and I flew to Madagascar to help re-open the Peace Corps program.

Transitioning to Madagascar had some bumps, for sure. I wasn't eager to learn another dialect (Malagasy). I was hesitant to make friends in my new village in case I was ripped out—forced to relocate—again. And my anti-malaria medication started wreaking havoc with my sleep, causing me to wake up with nightmares. But I remembered that ant and stuck it out.

I completed my Peace Corps duty and then crafted a plan to stay in-country and hike the length of Madagascar (another story that involves eight months, countless blisters and lemurs).

Along the way, I had an interesting—you might say life-changing or life-clarifying—encounter.

One day I stopped to take a photo of a woman sweeping her front yard with a bundle of strapped together banana leaves and corn husks. I greeted her. She looked at me, seemingly a little confused at seeing a 5'9" blonde woman walking through her village, but cheerfully answered my questions.

"How often do you sweep?" I asked her in Malagasy.

"Every morning, and sometimes in the evening." She answered.

"What do you usually sweep?"

"Whatever is on the ground. Usually husks, peels, and the occasional wrapper," the woman replied.

At that point, she gave me another quizzical but pleased look, probably curious why I asked such questions. I continued my inquiry, "And where do you put these sweepings?"

"Over there, across the road."

After a pause, I remarked, "I see you have a garden. Where do you get dirt for this garden?"

She replied, "Over there, across the road, at the bottom of the hill. That earth is 'cooked,' it's 'zezika.'" Zezika in Malagasy means compost.

I snapped her photo; we said our goodbyes and I practically skipped as I walked away, thinking, 'That was AWESOME. I learned about her waste-stream and how she composts. How wonderful!' Then, in the next moment, I shook my head at myself and thought, 'I am a freak. Who else gets this excited about trash?' I walked on and kept thinking about that conversation, about where I was, the things I had seen and done and was sure to see and do in the miles ahead. And it came to me. I should DO this. Like, really do this: I should work in the waste management industry. And thus, the seed of my career path sprouted.

I ended up spending 3+ years overseas, and that experience is embedded deep in my heart. I plan to go back some day to the people and places where I connected.

When I returned to the United States from Africa, I applied for a fellowship to travel the world and study garbage. The fellowship, which was established by the will of Alice Alvira Stevens, Wellesley class of 1891, states: "preference shall be given to persons with good temper and a natural generosity of view who when confronted with alien conditions, shows common sense in observing and comprehending social, economic, and political situations, a strong desire to travel, and a deep love of beauty."

> *"I often look down at my dusty feet and think, 'I have walked the length of this country with my right and left foot.' It made me connected to this country, and I've seen it just the way most of its population sees it."* And... *"Through [real] fire and through rain, I learned it's important to have fun along the way."*
> –Meredith (from one of the YouTube videos put together on return to the U.S.)

Earnest in my belief that proper waste management is not only beautiful but also integral to a sustainable future in the United States, I pitched my idea to spread my wings and see the world through the eyes of a waste-stream watcher, and bring that perspective back to the U.S. to share with our communities. But I didn't even make it to the interview round.

Resolute, I then enrolled in graduate school with a focus in garbology and landed a job managing the waste and recycling program for Portland International Airport, virtually a small city with 15 million passengers per year plus 40 food and beverage tenants. Over the next couple years, the tiny seedling of a career that was germinated by a serendipitous conversation with a woman sweeping by the side of the road grew into a dynamic tree of knowledge and experience. Let me push this metaphor too far. My work was rooted in data collection: my team and I would sort trash into material categories and identify opportunities to expand recycling. My interactions branched into almost every corner of the organization, from prep kitchens making gallons of coffee to janitorial staff collecting waste from a hurried audience to senior management reviewing hauling contracts, and so on. With creative juices flowing, I would synthesize our program into catchy stories. For example, the opening line of the first press release I ever wrote: "Alaska Airlines cares about ground control. Coffee ground control, that is," resulted in two TV stations covering coffee ground composting. With two years of this robust experience under my belt, I applied for the same fellowship and BOOM, I got it!

Thus, my early 30s were shaped by travel, including a 3-month bike trip from Mexico to Costa Rica, and trash (I visited landfills along the way).

Snapshots from 21 countries include: touring an anaerobic digester in Germany; videotaping collection trucks in Croatia; interning at Frankfurt International Airport; analyzing signage in Paris; attending a Food Waste Summit in Belgium; comparing the waste management programs (vastly different) and resulting recycling rates (strikingly similar) between Belgium and Guatemala; researching a landfill project in Nicaragua; re-entering the United States to serve as the keynote speaker for a recycling conference.

On my career path, I've been tempted by literal forks in the road. At one point, I became fascinated with Bob's Red Mill, a whole grain company based a few miles south of my new home. I also have a penchant for oats and a keen appreciation for how a bowl each morning can fuel my day. Finally, my friend lent me *People Before Profit*, Bob Moore's (the founder of Bob's Red Mill) book, and I was hooked. Here was a man who grew a company through hard work, determination, and giant, rotating rocks. He treated his employees well, made strategic donations throughout the community, and delivered top quality whole grain products.

I set up a meeting with the company's head of sales and marketing, Dennis Gilliam. I did my research and learned about some of his branding strategies using bow ties, and that he had a background in printing. As I walked up the stairwell, I was even more enamored by the company: thoughtful ads, glowing press reviews, and memorabilia lined the walls. In the waiting room, there was a touching photo album of the company's work with early childhood development and its link to nutrition.

Our meeting, late one afternoon, was in Dennis's large office, which felt more like a museum: print blocks, a manual corn shucking machine, and other knickknacks that all had a story were sprinkled throughout the space. We sat down and started chatting. Dennis said right out of the gate, "So you have a passion for whole grains?"

"Well, I eat oatmeal pretty much every single morning," I replied honestly.

With that unique opening, the conversation then continued along a lovely, gentle meander about oat preferences (Dennis likes steel cut; I prefer rolled) and travel (Bob's Red Mill had won the Scotland oat award).

But in the back of my head, his initial question nagged at me: Was I passionate about whole grains? I envisioned joining their stellar team. I imagined writing copy for their bags of product, or recipes, working in clever puns. And then realized I would likely be drawn to look in everyone's garbage can, as I tend to do wherever I am. I would then want to identify opportunities to reduce waste, then recycle. I realized, as much as I love my oats (and flax seed, quinoa, and other grains), that they are not my passion. So, I swung back to my roots. I wasn't as zealous about what grows in the ground as I was about what goes into the ground.

Like a planet getting pulled back into its correct gravitational force field, I returned to my work, promoting Harvest Power and its business of organic waste recycling, with even more zest. When I started working at Harvest, it was a company of ten employees with a bold vision. Over the next few years, it grew to $130-million in revenue with 450+ employees and locations across North America. In short, my job was to manage the company's profile, curate its image through marketing and communications, and identify creative ways to connect with local communities.

One of my favorite concoctions was creating flip flops that had a banana peel and apple core print, with the pun-laden call to action, "Step up to the plate: Recycle your organics."

The–ahem–appeal of inspiring food scrap composting on a national level mirrored my own path in my backyard. I was following in my parents' footsteps and had begun adding compost to my garden beds–dense clay when I moved in–each season. I distinctly remember glowing the day the Wall Street Journal carried an article on Harvest in its print edition, which is a milestone for anyone in media and marketing. That same evening as the sun was setting I went out into the garden and, for the first time in the years since I had begun adding compost to the super dense ground, I stepped onto my shovel and sunk completely into the fertile soil. It made a satisfying 'whoosh.' I felt so proud of my work on all levels, improving our footprints on the Earth.

I started my own company, Solid Strategies, with an intention to help organizations create fertile ground for a sustainable future. One of my main clients remains Harvest Power.

I had learned in life to follow my passion. I decided to keep doing what I loved and have developed a career and business that focuses on combining storytelling with waste management (recycling) and gardening (especially compost). And I cannot think of a better purpose in my life.

All lines connect, even if that connection is not always immediately apparent. I look at a globe of our Earth and how so many lines upon it converge and that its movement—rotation–turning endlessly, brings everything back to an observer's starting view. And so, it should be with what we produce and use throughout our lives on this planet. Our waste is a resource and not a by-product of human existence. Its end should transform into new beginnings, and that's a story I believe in passionately.

I feel successful when my professional and personal pursuits integrate into ways that feel nourishing. I prefer to think of work-life 'integration' contrasted with 'balance' as the latter, while a lovely aspiration, feels too fleeting. Work, to me, feels the most rewarding when producing great results and building meaningful relationships. Some of what I'm most proud of includes cultivating colleagues and industry professionals into mentors or friends. Play, to me, reaches its deepest enrichment when I can't distinguish between the two; when work and play become one. When you do what you love, time disappears. So, I gauge my success by how present I can be in the moment, whether I'm tackling a task, or interacting with a person, or simply being in a moment.

About Meredith Sorensen

Meredith is intimately familiar with environmental, social and economic issues related to recycling, renewable energy, and soil revitalization.

These topics spring to life through her contributed articles, displays, online media, smartphone applications, events, public speaking and print collateral.

Trash tells a story, and unlike most storytellers, it rarely lies. Increasing the sustainability of waste management has a profound effect on our global environment, economy, and attitude. For that reason, Meredith believes waste is beautiful. She loves to combine storytelling with waste management (recycling) and gardening (especially compost) to create compelling narratives about the beneficial impact to all individuals and citizens of our world.

Solid Strategies
WWW.SOLIDSTRATS.COM

As a consultant, Meredith is a single person business. She loves trash, the organic fraction of the waste-stream specifically. She helps companies tell the story of turning organic waste into clean energy and compost. She can't get over the number of conversations she has with people about trash and recycling. Not just the conversations she has with her colleagues, where talking trash is their job, but with the rest of the world that doesn't work in her industry. People, for the most part, care about our planet and want to find ways to exist on it without leaving a more damaging footprint. Solid Strategies works with companies to tell stories that evoke and support that sense of stewardship.

The Un-Sexy Entrepreneur

STEPHANIE WINANS

"I'm a good jumper, he said, but I'm not so good at landing. Maybe you should stay closer to the ground then, I said, and he shook his head and said the ground was the whole problem in the first place."
—BRIAN ANDREAS, FROM *STORY PEOPLE*

They say that the best products are born when entrepreneurs can't find an existing solution to a problem. And then those products often become the foundation of a business.

I think the same can be said for people and their careers or professions. If where you are (or aren't) in your career is a problem... perhaps because of someone else's rules, or you can't find a place—an employer—where you fit, or that will give you an opportunity, then create your own.

While I do believe companies in the United States are making giant strides forward, many mothers are still discriminated against in the workplace. And I wanted freedom from that feeling. When I decided to go out on my own, instead of working for someone else, it was because that decision solved a problem for me. I needed a job that met my desire to innovate in the digital media space and one that supported my role as a military wife who periodically had to relocate with her family. The problem I was solving wasn't an issue in the marketplace, but a personal career matter.

Not all entrepreneur stories are sexy: mine certainly isn't. It was a practical decision and calculated risk in betting on myself. I am what I like to call an 'accidental' entrepreneur.

Back in 2007, I worked for a broadcast media company and had started getting interest from clients about doing freelance work for them. That made me think about my options: I was concerned about my job, what career path was there for me with my employer and other issues of the flexibility I needed as a military spouse and mother.

It seemed that the interest from clients in me freelancing for them was a signal and one that I could not ignore. I resigned my position and started a small digital marketing agency, retaining that broadcast media company—my former employer—as my first large client. So, I left on good terms with them as a paying customer.

And the road it's taken me on has been a phenomenal experience!

* * *

Raised in Mobile, Alabama, I am a wife to a military pilot and a mother to two girls. I got married young and quickly realized that being a military spouse was a challenge I needed to accommodate with my career choices.

It's difficult to develop a career that doesn't lose traction with each move. I couldn't fathom the thought that when I had to relocate with my family, my employer wouldn't allow me to work remotely. My job duties and skills were such that they did not require me to be in a permanently fixed location. The work I performed certainly could have been done from a distance and that factored into my interest in entrepreneurship.

My decision to start my company was a leap of faith, an investment in myself and my family. I wanted to build a career that could sustain and progress even when moving every 3-4 years. Working for myself was a way to do that. I needed a career that didn't tie me to a geographic location but also wanted to build one that ensured I would never have to choose between roles—as a mother or an executive committed to my job.

Becoming a parent changes your perspective in so many ways, and that change in priorities is particularly challenging for women. I had a hard time at first finding my balance as a working mom. I never felt like I was doing it right. I constantly felt guilty and no one—work or my first child—was getting 100%. I felt like a failure. Angela Perelli, a life coach, and a friend helped me find my way. She told me to "keep my heart wherever my feet are" which motivated me to be fully present at work, and fully present at home. I still use this mantra today. She also taught me to treat my life as a job and learn how to prioritize and delegate. So, what if I can't handle working, grad school, and being a wife and mother? She empowered me to hire help where I needed it by delegating tasks that weren't a high priority and to stop apologizing for that.

It sounds simple, but my life hasn't been the same since these coaching sessions four years ago. Where did all that pressure to be perfect come from? I laugh now when I think about it, but that pressure was very real. Why don't more women share the struggles it takes to get to the successes? This was a big one for me. It took empowerment from a woman—and mom—I respected to help me find my footing as a working mother. Who says we can't do it all? And equally important, who says we must do it all? Defining our own rules is so important.

To other military spouses and mothers: you are a parent and a wife, but being there for your family does not mean you can't be devoted to your work. It doesn't have to be a mutually exclusive proposition.

If the path you're on isn't taking you where you want to go, then create a new one that will. Maybe that's entrepreneurship, and maybe it's changing industries... or maybe it's just having a conversation with your current or prospective employer about your needs. I know that the solution you seek is out there, from my own experience. Ultimately, when I was at that crossroads and torn in two directions, what I discovered was that I could not keep playing by someone else's rules. That feeling of uncertainty, day after day, drove me to change my circumstances and create the conditions to become free. I made my own rules.

* * *

The truth is that I started a business because the opportunity fell in my lap. But I believe that opportunities are presented to you when you are ready to act on them. There's a saying that 'fortune favors the prepared,' and I was ready!

My focus initially was on radio and entertainment, and I particularly enjoyed working with corporations launching new stations and new shows. I found the up and coming—emerging—clients were much more exciting to work with than people and companies who were already on top. I soon had several entrepreneurial clients, using my skills for launching new media brands to develop go-to-market strategies for their startup companies. That's how I fell in love with helping other people launch new brands and being scrappy to fight for market share.

One of the companies I began working with was Bundoo. When I got involved, it was in the ideation phase. The company was brand new, just finishing initial consumer research and in the early stages of product development, and Bundoo's founder was looking for someone to build a go-to-market strategy. I was attracted to the idea and excited at the challenge of building a business in a very, very crowded market. But just like the decision to start my company, Bundoo was a big leap of faith, too. I believe it will become a household name, one trusted by parents and recommended by pediatricians and OB/GYNs. Bundoo will be THE health resource for expecting and new moms and THE resource recommended by physicians.

At Bundoo my passion for the business blossomed and my duties soon increased. I took on increasingly larger roles and responsibility, progressing from Marketing Manager to Vice President, and eventually CEO. And as CEO, one of my key responsibilities was to secure funding for the company. Raising capital is an emotional ride. You book meetings, and you never know what kind of investor you're going to get. There are the guys (and by guys, I mean both men and women) who talk to you like you're an idiot because the funding pitches feed their power tripping egos, and there are the guys who treat you with respect but push you as hard as you can to see if you'll break. And then there are the investors who are real leaders and mentors to the investment and entrepreneurial communities. When you have calls with each type in one day, it's tough! You don't know walking in what kind of person you'll get and what kind of experience you'll have. You don't have time to be distracted by your emotions: fear, respect, awe, and in some cases self-preservation, disgust, and anger. Doing this for months, day in and day out, you're eventually running on adrenaline.

Securing backing for Bundoo was hard. We're a healthcare-based consumer business with a niche focus on women and a hybrid business model. To say we needed the right investor was an understatement! We have ultimately been successful because I refused to give up and because I have thick skin. I started each day with the same goal: end the day with confidence that I had worked as hard as possible to ensure the company's financial stability. I didn't let myself get distracted by the rude and disrespectful investors met.

Along the way, we hit a major hurdle. Running short of capital, we needed to scale back operations. I had to do the one thing I never dreamed would happen, let my team go. One by one, I called the people who built Bundoo and broke the news. They had two weeks, and then they wouldn't have jobs. And worse, I had to admit that the future of the company was uncertain.

We'd spent three years building a resource beloved by parents and healthcare providers. How was it possible that we wouldn't be successful? I made a promise to them that I would continue to devote 100% of my time to gaining stability with the hopes of giving them their jobs back, but asked that they move on for their personal best interests. It was heartbreaking. They weren't even angry. Instead, they were crying for me and the burden I was carrying, I just couldn't take it. How could this team be so loyal to our mission and me even when I was delivering the worst news for them and their families? Their support fueled my determination. And like an episode of the hit show *Silicon Valley*, we began the craziest rollercoaster ride. Two weeks later, I had secured a strategic acquirer, and I offered them their jobs back. It was the happiest day of my professional life. Running a startup is hard, but I found that with the lowest valleys came the highest peaks. It's been a surreal success story for our team.

I could give you a lot of general advice about having a plan or a vision, then executing the plan without losing sight of that vision. Or about faith, which can carry you a long way and get you through difficult and troubling times. But frankly, you can get that in a lot of books, magazines, and business related sites online. What I want to share with you is something that I don't hear—read or see—discussed often.

If you're considering starting your own business, get inspired by the un-sexy entrepreneurs: the owners of mom and pop shops in your city, the freelancers who sustain their families by word of mouth business. It's daunting to be inspired by the Richard Bransons and Elon Musks of the world. Not all of us will invent the next Tesla, but each of holds our own magic within and has gifts to give to the world. The inspiration for entrepreneurship is all around you; you just have to look for it. There's a stirring essay, *Acres of Diamonds,* now 103 years old, that has inspired hundreds of thousands—maybe millions—of entrepreneurs. The premise of the story is that one need not look elsewhere for opportunity, achievement, or fortune, the resources to achieve all good things are present in your community. I'll add to that by saying that, you... yourself... are the primary resource for finding your opportunities in life and business. Start there.

Success—to me—is a balance scale that has two variables and two outcomes:

- *The person using it.*
- *What goes on each side of the scale.*
- *Whether the scale is balanced or tilted.*
- *How that—the balance or imbalance—makes the person feel.*

Success—what you define as it for yourself—goes on one side of the scale. You choose what goes on the other side. For me it's my family, a career I can devote my talents to, time for personal hobbies and giving back. My goal is to reach the balance point where all is even. Defining what that balance means to you requires some flexibility to let that definition ebb and flow, it can change over time. The ultimate reward is when you see the success—what qualifies it for you—rising higher. That means you are leveraging all that you put into life—into creating what you want for yourself—to the maximum degree. The sum of the whole is greater than the parts, and so everything tilts more in your favor. Success is different for each of us. Your scale may hold different things, and your balance may not look like mine. But knowing you hold that scale in your hand, choosing what to put on it, and owning the outcome—to me, that's success.

About Stephanie Winans

Stephanie is responsible for planning and developing long-term growth strategies, as well as staff management and day-to-day operations at Bundoo. Previously, she worked in the radio and music industries creating digital strategies for talent, becoming an entrepreneur, writer, and public speaker along the way. Recently completing an MBA at the University of North Carolina at Chapel Hill, Stephanie holds a Bachelor's of Science degree in marketing and psychology from Spring Hill College.

Bundoo
WWW.BUNDOO.COM

Bundoo makes the Internet reliable for parents. They are the only physician-driven pregnancy and parenting site where expecting and new parents can interact directly with doctors and healthcare experts and get the actionable information they can trust. Bundoo bridges the gap between physicians and parents with a reference library full of articles written or reviewed by doctors and healthcare experts, private ask-the-doctor telehealth service and expert-moderated social community. Their experts are U.S. credentialed, actively practicing, up-to-date on current research and recommendations, and passionate about educating parents.

Pushing Through Barriers
DAN CALDWELL

*"Success is my only motherf****n' option, failure's not..."*
—EMINEM, FROM *LOSE YOURSELF*

I thought of my daughter. The back of my hand gripping the steering wheel was wet from wiping my eyes so I could see. Light through the van's windshield glistened on it as I reached to turn up the music. Eminem's song, *Lose Yourself* blasted—an anthem, a soundtrack for my life—twisting me inside. Its lyrics, his voice—the way he delivered the song—hurt: "Fact... that I can't provide the right type of life for my family...." A song can bring back memories, make you laugh, make you happy... but they can also bring pain, make you feel trapped and hopeless because you see yourself in the song.

Caged inside my head, I drove on—thinking about my daughter—staring at the road ahead through tears. I wasn't scared of failure. That's not what made me cry. I had so many people depending on me... and no one else in my family was going to be the one to pull us up from where we were. I could not let them down, it was all on me. That energy is what drove me, but sometimes all the worries and questions piled on. That's the reason for the tears. I started yelling—louder than the music—at myself... "I'm gonna make it...."

I leaned forward and punched the windshield. "I'm gonna make it." When my hand went back on the steering wheel, there in the glass was now a four or five-inch crack. It remained there for as long as I owned that van (and sometimes I wonder if it still has it), a constant reminder that it was up to me to do things right, get things done. Failure was not an option. I fed on that energy, and that's what got me through. It's what kept me going.

* * *

Daymond John, Founder of FUBU, who while working shifts at Red Lobster took a simple idea and created what is now a billion-dollar brand, once said: "Poor people put a low value on themselves and their efforts." Some people—especially those who fall into the category he mentions—might read that quote from him and think it's certain: 'That's all they can be... that's all they'll ever be.' They're not worthy and destined to be unsuccessful, why try. Daymond is someone I admired and was actually a role model of mine when starting my company TapouT. I understand what he means, but questioned it. I didn't accept and buy into what he said.

Certainly, not when it came to me and to those I talk to today.

As a teen in high school, I would often skip school and drive the Pacific Coast Highway (PCH). Along the road, I would see large stunning houses. So many that it made me think, 'How can someone get to the point where they have such a nice house to live,'— looking through the car window at the coast streaming by or curving just ahead of me—'where they can live in this beautiful spot.' I wondered, 'Are those houses just for the privileged?' Which made me think of people like me. Where I came from was far from privilege and light years away from the houses on the PCH. But there were so many of them, not all those houses had to be owned by people born rich, and that told me it could be done.

Uncomfortable with how things were, I endlessly soul-searched and studied to figure a way out, to get to where I wanted to be. What helped was reading stories about successful people, but not just those who had what I would call an average or easy climb to success; those who benefited from a solid foundation and clear path to follow. I enjoyed most the stories about those who struggled. Don't tell me that the road is hard... the journey long. I knew that then and know it now. Give me a story about someone who scrapped and fought their way up and over the mountain to get to the other side; and that they sweated and bled along the way. Don't jump to the 'they lived happily ever after' ending. I needed—wanted—to see the details how they made it through all of the hardships to get to what they consider success. It was important for me to see and read about people more like me. Those born without a silver spoon in their mouth, who from unfortunate circumstances, harsh surroundings and without any resources other than their own willpower, became successful.

A lot of people love that iconic picture of Michael Jordan, from one of the NBA Slam Dunk competitions, where he's soaring, effortlessly, to the basket. I appreciate it and the imagery, but my favorite picture of Jordan is one where he's got his hands on his knees. Sweat running down his face... dripping from him, streams of it down his neck, shoulders, and arms. Jersey stuck to his chest, even in that static image you can tell he's breathing deep, nearly spent. He's given everything and left it on the court.

In that picture—in his eyes—you can see the thousands of hours of practice it took to get to where he was. All the tears, sweat and even blood he paid out—body and soul—to become a great basketball player. That's the cost of commitment I understand. No easy street. No quick path to stardom, to success. It's doing the time, doing the reps... it's gutting through all the bad just to reach the good. Show me how that works, and I can do it. I have done it.

I've always been fascinated by what happens when someone does what was thought to be impossible. As a young man, I wasn't sure I would ever break records or do the impossible but knew—with rock-solid certainty—that I could do what others had done. If I could see that then, some way if I kept trying... I could do it, too. Back then I wasn't the smartest guy in the room, but I knew I could start a business and follow other successes. One particular story that I read really struck home how valid that belief was.

On May 6, 1954, Roger Bannister did something no one ever in history had officially done before when the announcer covering the one-mile race declared: "The time was three--," then the cheers of the crowd drowned out Bannister's exact time, which was 3 min 59.4 sec. Though many—including experts—believed it was impossible for the human body to run that fast, the spectators had just witnessed the world's first official sub-4-minute mile.

Bannister had relentlessly visualized that achievement to make his mind and body actually do it. His record lasted just 46 days. The important message to take away from his accomplishment is not that he broke the record. It is that others broke it so soon afterward. It adds to my point that there is strength in knowing something can be done. That's what gets you through.

But here's why some people don't succeed. If they can't get someone to tell them all they have to do is just try… if they can't get a guarantee that if they put in the effort, then they'll win. Then they don't play—they don't attempt it. I was willing to do it—start my business—on the chance that I could make it. The doing of what most people won't is the difference between those who succeed (eventually) and those who do not.

That one simple premise—believing that what I wanted to accomplish was possible if others had done it—is what continually prodded and sustained me early on. And now, I know that no matter what I take on I have within me the power to succeed. I was willing to do what was needed, to gut it out, as long as what I'm trying to do is possible. Not easy. Possible.

With any obstacle, ways to get over through or around it begins simply with this: starting. And the first things you try likely won't work. Sometimes you must experiment and gain experience. Life's about finding—sometimes creating—then going after and acting on opportunities. Then with that opportunity in front of you, it's like being in a competition… sometimes against other people, sometimes against situations or circumstances.

That's the way it is for most of us, and that's certainly been the case in my life. But my toughest competition has always been myself. Maybe my worst personal beat down, the bottom, was when I didn't make it as a police officer. The thoughts running through my head at that moment the department let me go—the kind that haunts you and never seems to let go—were so familiar. They had been with me most of my life. I wasn't good enough. I just didn't fit in. I was my own enemy... I knew I had to overcome that but just did not know how.

* * *

Growing up in San Bernardino California, my parents didn't have a lot of money, but I didn't know that because I had such a great childhood. It wasn't until I was a little older and realized that some of my friends had nicer houses, cars, and better clothes. They were solidly middle-class and we—my family—were not. I began to feel out of place. Maybe some kids made fun of me, or maybe I was just more aware of what was different between us, but once I realized how my friends lived—what they had that I did not—I started a lifelong journey of entrepreneurialism.

In elementary school, probably around fifth grade, I sold candy and marbles to the other kids. We used to all play marbles during lunch, and I could usually sell my marbles for three or four times what I paid for them at the store. I saved the change earned in those transactions in a small plastic container shaped like a tooth. Sometimes I would skip eating lunch so that I could save that money too. I don't remember what I bought with the money but liked creating ways to make it.

During that time, my neighborhood was somewhat decent with mostly lower-middle-class families. Then gangs, mostly Crips and Bloods from Los Angeles, started moving into the area and taking over. Once, when I was around 12 years old, in the middle of the night, I woke to the sound of a series of bangs on my bedroom wall that faced the street. My dad ran in and pulled me out of my bed onto the floor and laid on top of me. "Dad!" I asked him. "What's going on? Why's someone hitting the walls with a hammer?"

"It's okay, Dan, just stay down. It's shooting."

The next morning, we found out it was AK47 fire—spewed up and down the street—that had killed someone ten doors down. There were a bunch of other incidents but even with all of that I never really felt in danger. Even after a break-in at our house when my dad, my brother and I were shot at, I still never felt afraid to go outside. I guess that was just our 'normal,' and something we got accustomed to.

When I was in eighth grade, our school didn't have a lot of money and put out a bulletin looking for a DJ that would be cheaper than hiring who they had in the past. My friend Philip and I immediately went to the principal and told him that we were DJs. Of course, we weren't and didn't know anything about DJ'ing other than we had seen them at our school previously. We remembered all the girls hanging around the DJs, and that was intriguing to teenage boys. We used all our parent's stereo equipment and went out and bought a bunch of albums for our first dance. We learned on the job, and it eventually became a pretty good business! With our earnings, we bought the best equipment we could afford and tons of lighting. We became known for the show we put on because we had lasers, fog machines and lights that were synchronized to the beat of the music. We reinvested profits to have the equipment to do what our competition could not do. The other schools in our district began to hire us, and even some that were outside our area. Every weekend we had a dance booked and charged several hundred dollars for the two-hour dance.

I remember once, at one of our gigs, going out on the floor to check the lights and sound—how everything looked from that viewpoint—and from way in the back I looked out over the crowd of people. This strong feeling came over me, 'They're here because of us… and are having fun.' That gave me my first taste of what it's like to be proud of something that I had a hand in creating, that amped up sense of gratification. Though I didn't recognize what Phillip and I were doing was a business, it was. And I learned so much from it that helped me realize I could create my own opportunities and do good things. Even though I was fairly popular, I didn't hang out with the in-crowd, the cool kids. My friend Phillip and I were loners, and though I always felt insecure and didn't feel like I fit in, I made it through okay.

In 1993, I was 22 years old, and my friend Charles and I were training to be police officers. We had watched the first Ultimate Fighting Championship (UFC) and noticed this guy, Royce Gracie who had fought three times in a single night and won each match. He was smaller than his opponents and still managed to win. That resonated with me because I'm relatively short. He used a grappling technique that we recognized would be a more effective way to deal with a combative suspect than what we were being trained on. We tracked him down and a week later began training with Royce at his studio in Torrance, California. We fell in love with what he taught us—the sport of Jiu Jitsu—and it was all we could talk or think about. We wanted to devote all our time to become more proficient and also got hooked on the UFC events.

Back then, Mixed-Martial Arts (MMA) was still a new thing—an almost underground sport—that was illegal in 48 states. Nobody believed in it. Even politicians like John McCain felt it was too brutal and should remain illegal. The sport was (and is) primal—far more so than boxing—and tapped something at the core of many people. That heart pounding, feet-shifting, body-conscious sense of almost being in the fight that lasted the duration of the bout as you watched skilled, professional, fighters in the arena. My friends and I felt it in our bones. I saw that same feeling in the faces and body language of hundreds, then thousands of fans.

We'd see the fighters selling their t-shirts at their gyms and training centers and that interested us. We had a conversation with Royce about how many shirts the Gracie's were selling and wondered if that could be replicated but with a brand that was more universal and geared toward both Jiu Jitsu and MMA and didn't cater to any single training center or fighter. My company was the first to sell t-shirts as a real business using a sales system at the events. They became ubiquitous in the industry.

The sport was so unknown that it was well under the radar of other apparel companies. But we had seen how much the fans were into it. We were sure that anybody who enjoyed training or watching UFC, admiring the toughness of the fighters and the sport, would want our t-shirts. I knew that what we wanted to do to be a part of the sport, starting a business aligned with it, would be huge. We would hit it big. That filled me with a certainty so powerful, that when I was pitching people—whether on the business itself or just the sport—I gave everything that was in me. I gave it my all.

Despite my parent's misgivings, in 1997, my friend Charles Lewis and I—both of us without college degrees and little money—started a company we named TapouT (in MMA when your opponent 'taps out,' you win). By 'little money'... I mean zero. I maxed out two credit cards: one with a $5000 limit and the other with a $10,000 limit. That's what bankrolled us in the beginning. Our friend Tim Katz joined us in 1999. We all had trained in MMA and were not only ardent fans of the sport but also disciples telling others about it. Living and breathing it, everyone we introduced to MMA became instant fans. We were confident that someday it would become wildly popular. And we would be attached at the hip to this emerging sport! We took a leap of faith that most people are unwilling to do.

I can remember in the early stage of starting the business—probably for the first six years or so—we wanted to appear like a bigger company than we were. We had gotten to the point where we were sponsoring fighters in the UFC who appeared on pay-per-view television. People didn't know we were paying what we could afford—up to $1,000 per fighter—because these guys were not making very much for their fights and we wanted to support them and the sport. Everyone thought we were this big multi-million-dollar company when were just doing what we could within our means at the time. Sometimes with the larger payouts, we had to make installments payments to the fighters. Looking at it practically to make that perception work for us, we wanted to have a 24-hour customer service line—just like the big retailers—that could take orders around the clock.

That customer service line was me, my cell phone, and order forms that I kept folded in my back pocket. At the time, I was also working two full-time jobs: as a police officer and as a security guard. I would have these order forms on me at all times and often got calls while at work. I had set up the phone line so that when a call came in, if not at home to take it, the call would forward to my cell phone. We tried not to miss any phone calls, but it happened sometimes. If I missed a call on my cell phone, it would forward to an answering service that would take the order. However, this was very expensive costing us around three dollars per minute. After I got off both jobs, I would fulfill orders.

One evening, probably in 2000, I remember being so tired, I was only getting two or three hours of sleep a day, that I crashed my car on the freeway driving home from work after falling asleep at the wheel. Not long afterward, I was on a night shift and in a parking lot trying to sneak in a few minutes of sleep since work was slow. I guess my phone rang or I thought it had and I answered the police microphone saying, "TapouT Clothing!" Which was how I would answer the phone believing it was an order coming through. A fellow police officer, who knew my situation, came back over the police radio and jokingly told me, "Wrong phone!" I didn't live that down for a while.

By 2005, the UFC had grown much larger, so they decided to do a reality show called *The Ultimate Fighter*. We did everything we could to get our clothes in the show, without paying of course! At the end of the season, they held a finale for the show that consisted of a live fight between the two contestants that had successfully fought through all the episodes. They also had a super fight between two regular UFC fighters.

We worked out a trade with the UFC for clothing as a sponsorship deal to have our logo on the mat, and a small spot that would air on television. At the end of the show (which was absolutely fantastic) one of the UFC guys told us:

"10 million viewers are watching this!"

Up until then, events had only drawn around 200,000 viewers. That's when I received a call from my website guy.

"Your site is crashing. You're getting around 3,000 orders an hour. Some users can't place orders cause the servers can't handle the volume!"

We were losing business but overall making more sales than we ever had in our history.

On the fly, we scrambled to figure out a solution and ended up shutting off the processing of credit cards, to free up system resources to only capture the order information. This was a good and bad thing because while the system would most likely catch all the orders, we had no inventory system to tell us if the product was in stock or not. At that volume, we were running out of everything. On top of that, later we would need to manually process each order. Overall this would seem like good problems to have, and they were, but when they say that success can cripple you, I know exactly what they mean.

Over the next three months, we handled thousands of customer service calls from customers wondering where their orders were and trying to compensate them for the delay. All while trying to produce as much as we could, as fast as we could.

Then the credit card company shut us down, accepting orders but not giving us the proceeds—money—that we desperately needed for production. Because we were self-capitalized, this was a game ender! Without money, we were dead in the water. The credit card processing company we were using claimed we weren't qualified to do that amount of business, having been only approved for up to $50,000 a month in sales. Now, I believe that selling $400,000 in a month was a good thing and what we were supposed to do as a business. But they were penalizing us for it!

I called Charles to let him know I didn't know how to get out of this situation. He answered his phone and let me vent, then told me, "Just last week we met with that businessman who has built successful businesses before, and he's interested in what we're doing. Maybe you should call him."

At that point, I didn't have anything to lose, hung up and immediately dialed this businessman. Within a 15-minute conversation, I convinced him to cosign for us at the credit card company for sales of up to $500,000 a month. Shortly afterward, we were able to get all our money and get back on track to deliver goods to all our customers. It was a ton of work getting caught up, but we did it.

I remember vividly one time when we had a special warehouse sale. When it started, I watched—completely blown away—as the lines grew and stretched outside to wind around the building. Then it began to rain. And the people stayed in line, patiently working their way forward to come in and buy our shirts and products. We scrambled to take care of them and had workers go to nearby stores and buy all the umbrellas they could get, bringing them back to hand to our customers waiting in the rain. That moment, like what I had experienced back in school as a DJ, but far greater, was this tremendous sense of delivering something good and valuable. For me, that is the best feeling in the world.

Each year got increasingly better. We faced—and dealt with—challenges like most companies do, especially those growing as fast as TapouT. I had a lot to learn but did so in the best possible environment—day-to-day business.

One day in 2009, I was at the gym working out in the morning before going into the office. The company was doing amazingly well. We had our own TV show (and had just negotiated the third season) and were selling hundreds of millions of dollars' worth of products. The day before we had done an amazing photo shoot with our Ferraris, Lamborghinis and classic cars—all fruits of our labor—for the cover of Dub Magazine. That morning at the gym I got a text message from a fighter friend of mine that lived in Huntington Beach. It said something like, "Do you, or any of your guys, own a red Ferrari?"

I texted back, "Charles does. Why?" My partner, Charles also lived in Huntington Beach.

He replied, "I think you should check into a crash that happened last night... I think it might have been him."

Charles had driven his Ferrari home that evening after the photo shoot, and I guess decided to go to the gym later that night. He was hit by a drunk driver and killed.

After this, the company went on but my heart just wasn't in it, and I decided to sell the business.

There were a bunch of other factors involved, but I realized without that passion—like when Charles and I had started the company—it just wasn't the same. You see ultimately, we weren't doing this for the money. The money was nice, but we enjoyed every minute of everything that we did and that made us relentless. Take away that passion, and you just have a business that makes money. That might be great for some people, but it isn't what drives me.

In 2010, I sold the company and continued as president for another five years before leaving to find a new passion. I learned that passion is what gets you up without your alarm clock. It's what won't let you fall asleep because you can't stop thinking about ideas. It's what gives you that edge over the competition. That is what separates you from the guys that will fail. It's a small advantage but makes all the difference.

THE MAN IN THE ARENA
Theodore Roosevelt

Excerpt from the speech *Citizenship in A Republic* delivered at the Sorbonne, in Paris, France on 23 April 1910:

"It is not the critic who counts; not the man who points out how the strong man stumbles, or where the doer of deeds could have done them better. The credit belongs to the man who is actually in the arena, whose

face is marred by dust and sweat and blood; who strives valiantly; who errs, who comes short again and again, because there is no effort without error and shortcoming; but who does actually strive to do the deeds; who knows great enthusiasms, the great devotions; who spends himself in a worthy cause; who at the best knows in the end the triumph of high achievement, and who at the worst, if he fails, at least fails while daring greatly, so that his place shall never be with those cold and timid souls who neither know victory nor defeat."

At the time, some people talked negatively about me selling the company but they have never walked in my shoes, and they don't know what I know. It was time for TapouT to move forward without me. Like your son or daughter that turned 18 and went off to college. I enjoy seeing it move forward but I also believe that TapouT will not be the biggest thing I ever do. Since leaving TapouT, I've had the chance to do a lot of soul-searching. I'm looking for that next big adventure and have my hands in a lot of different things right now trying to find where that next passion leads me. I've invested in new products, patents, real estate and emerging markets. One of my projects that keep me up at night is something I started with my wife called, Billionaire Collectibles. She's an amazing entrepreneur too, who founded a multimillion-dollar company of her own. I'm so glad we could create a new business and venture together. It's something every entrepreneur needs. I have found that fire again and can't wait to let the world in on it. I'm just excited about life and where it will lead!

When I'm asked for advice, I usually can't give anything specific because everyone's journey is different. But the basics apply to everybody. Life is short, and before you know it, you will be at its end. Looking back on your life, ask yourself if you have any regrets. If you have a dream, you need to chase it down with a sense of urgency and with everything that you have in you! Time is the most precious thing on Earth, and you can never get it back. We have only one chance at this thing, to be exactly the person that we see ourselves as or at least die trying. I'm still—in part—the guy who failed as a police officer, that fifth-grader who felt ashamed that morning his mom dropped him off in a spitting and sputtering old rust bucket, that guy whose toughest opponent was himself. But I'm also the guy who pushed through doubt and insecurities to find and define my passion, and that's what led me to success, that's how I see myself.

Every single one of us can push past failure and can achieve what we once thought was impossible.

I refuse to have regrets. I want to be right in all parts of my life, with family and opportunities. To me that's success.

About Dan Caldwell

In 1997, Dan and his partner Charles put what little money they had together and formed the apparel company TapouT. Dan has been featured on CNN, FOX Business, Bloomberg News, a CNBC Business Special, a Tony Robbins infomercial, Forbes, INC. Magazine, The Wall Street Journal, and even a character in a video game. He has acted in and produced movies, having worked on Lionsgate's *Warrior*, among others, as well as the TapouT TV series, which aired on Versus (now NBC Sports). He is also the host of the TapouT radio show on SiriusXM.

As a youth growing up in a poor neighborhood in San Bernardino, California, Dan had no real mentors to look up to. Because of this, it has become his passion to make an impact on students' lives. In 2009, his business partner was killed by a drunk driver, but before passing, he wrote: "It may not be me that touches a million people, but maybe I'll touch that one that reaches a million!"

Dan believes this to be his mission in life. A Southern California resident, and proud father of four, Caldwell now speaks to thousands every year, traveling around the world and inspiring others through his amazing story.

TapouT
WWW.TAPOUT.COM

TapouT is an American multinational corporation that designs and manufactures sports clothing, casual apparel, and accessories. Following the growing popularity of mixed-martial arts in the United States, and its later mainstream acceptance, it became the largest MMA-related merchandise company in the world. In March 2015, the company was relaunched following its acquisition by entertainment company WWE and development firm Authentic Brands Group. It is now one of the largest sportswear manufacturers in the United States, and one of the biggest in the world.

ROBIN BEHRSTOCK

PART II

"Either you run the day or the day runs you."
—JIM ROHN

Something I've learned is that once you've found your path, you must be persistent and make sacrifices to reach your goal. This means working on your business when everyone else is sleeping or playing. Stand quietly yet boldly resolute before those that doubt you. Deal with self-doubts by doing the work, whatever it may be. Action can and will handle self-doubts. Make it happen. Learn to welcome criticism because it will surely come. When it happens, take anything from it that you can to learn and improve or get better, and let go of the rest. Do the work. Hone your craft. Take a risk. Learn what you need to move your life in the direction you want. If it's important enough to you... you'll find a way.

> *"The most effective way to do it...*
> *is to do it."*
> —Amelia Earhart

After several attempts and ventures, I found what worked for me. I had built a business that grew and thrived. I was living my dream and loving it, but still wanted to peel back the layers—of my personal feelings—and open up but felt changes in my life were necessary for me to be truly happy. With my business stable and growing, it was time to give that a try.

I was inspired by someone I met at an e-commerce conference, named David, who had been living in and working from an Airstream trailer (the kind you pull behind a vehicle) for two years, traveling with his wife and toddler. I wondered if I could do the same. Could I live on the road and run my business at the same time? Life would be so simple with no set plans or commitments. In my 'normal' life, I was always running from one activity or meeting to the next, not fully engaged because I spread myself too thin. While trying to focus on one thing, I was busy anticipating the next. I thought back to what David was doing with his life and was inspired.

Airstreams are silver, but I thought I could buy one and paint it a copper color, work from the road, visit customers, market to new ones, and it would be a great brand awareness campaign. I knew I needed to do it sooner rather than later, while nothing was holding me back. I began to scheme and realized I couldn't tow an Airstream with my Subaru Outback, and a motorhome would be a lot easier to drive. I also considered that when traveling solo, driving a fancy copper Airstream could make me target for any number of unfortunate incidents. I decided to go with a small motorhome that I could brand with my logo and planned to hit the road in early May of 2016.

I have always felt that I am living to the fullest when traveling. There's something about it that's harmonious for me. There are times when things slowed down, and I thought if I could do it for long enough and spend more time reflecting, hopefully, I could be better at finding deeper connections with people met along the way or friends who joined me for part of the journey. I thought, why not do that—travel—for an extended period?

That might sound self-centered, and a means to escape from real life. But a wise friend once told me: "Travel is not selfish, it helps us learn who we are so we can be more passionate about realizing what is important to us, and effective in achieving it. Our travels can inspire others to do the same—to see the world—and gain perspective. And perspective is what enables us to appreciate all the great things about being alive and living in a free country full of the comforts of a modern world."

I was and still am grateful to have the freedom to roam, and to have created a business that can be managed from anywhere. The startup phase was exciting, and I didn't mind the long hours involved. I liked owning a small business that could be operated from anywhere with two employees who loved their jobs. It's a common saying, 'sink or swim' and I knew I needed to continue to grow if I wanted my business to thrive despite the increasing competition.

However, after three years, I did not feel completely fulfilled. My favorite part of being an entrepreneur was (and still is) inspiring people. Selling copper mugs was not what I wanted to do the rest of my life. So, I decided to put my company on the market for sale shortly before hitting the road. Whether I sold the business or not didn't matter since I could run it from anywhere.

I hired a business broker, gave him financial reports and details about the business, and he listed it for sale. It wasn't too long before the broker advised me of some inquiries about my business. One of them resulted in a great phone call with a small private equity firm (a company whose purpose is to buy or invest in other businesses). They said one of their partners would be in Denver the next day and we made plans to meet for lunch.

We talked about our entrepreneurial journeys and how his firm's experience could be a good fit to take my business to the next level. We had a great conversation, and by the time I looked up, four hours had gone by. Their interest in my business and what they planned to do with it seemed like a good fit with what I wanted. I was excited about the great connection and invited him to see my new tiny home—my Winnebago RV—and meet my employee Lisa. Later that day, I finished packing up my life and hit the open road. The first stop was Cheyenne, Wyoming, only two hours away.

NOTABLE EXPERIENCES ON THE ROAD

After about five days on the road solo, I started feeling lonely, so I went to a local pub in Lander, Wyoming with the hopes of finding good conversation and making new friends. I met Zach, who had recently moved from Denver to build a house for his parents and help his sister-in-law, Wendy, take care of her two-year-old and two-month-old. Zach's younger brother Jon (Wendy's husband), had recently died in a climbing accident.

I enjoyed getting to know Zach. He took me on a drive up to what the locals called 'the sinks.' As we approached them, he said, "Watch this," and pointed through the window. A raging river had been paralleling the road, and suddenly it dipped down and disappeared!

"Where'd the river go?" I turned in my seat to look at him, not exactly sure what I had just seen.

He smiled and nodded toward the windshield, gesturing ahead of us on down the road but didn't answer me. We had gone about a quarter of a mile when the river surged back above ground and roared down its channel and off into the distance.

Zach grinned at me and slowed down, pulling over to the side of the road. "Years ago, they put dye in the water to run a test to get an idea of where the water traveled before it comes back up. It took several hours for the dyed water to come out." He pointed at where the torrent came out of the ground. "The water goes deep into the Earth before making it back to the surface."

I was amazed and for a minute, thought about how were it not for deciding to make this trip, I would never have seen it, and wondered about what else I would get to see.

"Do you want to get some pizza?" Zach asked.

I looked at my watch, it was close to dinner time. "Yeah, and then I need to find a place to park overnight."

"No problem, we'll eat and then you can follow me and park your RV outside my apartment complex. It's big enough, and no one will bother you."

The next morning, he knocked on my door. "Want to join us for breakfast? We're making pancakes!"

"Sure," I followed him to his apartment. There I met Wendy and her two young children. She was constantly breastfeeding both. I had no idea how she could find time for a job with all of that breastfeeding and taking care of her kids. That's why she needed Zach's help.

It was cool to see a family that just hung around the house, bonding with the babies and nothing else planned for the entire day. It was far different than how I was raised and how I'm geared. I was always taught to be busy, accomplish things, plan and work to get rich, etc., but Wendy had none of those thoughts on her mind. What fulfilled her was nourishing her babies and giving them the attention and love they needed. That decision to focus only on being a mother is just as admirable as concentrating on career and making money. Of course, money is needed to provide for your family and thank goodness Wendy had supportive family like Zach helping her.

Later that day it was time for me to move on. I thanked Zach and Wendy and then got back on the road. I had 160 miles to go to my next stop, north on Highway 287 to west on US-26 until it turned into Highway 191 to take me to Jackson, Wyoming.

It rained most of the way. Entering the town on rain-slick streets, I found a coffee shop to work from for a couple of hours. Then I drove around and found a hiking trail, worked some more and then decided to go to a local brewery for happy hour. I sat at the bar and started chatting with the guy next to me, a firefighter named Andy. We talked for a while then he asked, "Do you want to see some more spots around town? I have a tandem bike we can ride around on."

"Sure!" I finished my drink and off we went riding around Jackson, hipster style. I'm always super-cautious, and this was no different. I had told him about my business and road trip and before I left him he offered, "If you need some desk space to work at tomorrow, you can come over to my place while I study for an EMT test."

The next morning, I worked from his home, and that day I received the Letter of Intent from the private equity firm I had met with the week before. They liked my business more than similar companies due to its diversification: a strong Amazon presence, a strong brand and website sales, a solid customization side of the business and plenty of potential to grow. My business was now under contract to sell! I would continue to run it as usual and would work with them on due diligence, providing all the business financial data, analytics, lists and any other information they needed to confirm they would move forward with the purchase.

I continued traveling westward. In Spokane, I picked up six friends at the airport, and we headed for the Gorge Amphitheater in my Winnebago for a music festival. The Gorge is considered one of the most scenic concert venues in the world. The 27,500-seat outdoor concert venue is near the Columbia River and has sweeping and majestic views as it skirts the foothills of the Cascade Mountain Range. Its spectacular views of the Columbia Gorge canyon are breathtaking.

The next day, as we listened to wonderful live music, my friend Drew and I went to a deck that looked out over the gorge. I started talking with a nearby group of three friends: Dave, his wife Elisa and their friend

JJ. I took a photo of them, then I got in the picture and had someone else take one of all of us. Then that person got in the picture, and so on. What started as three people turned into a photo of twelve! We talked about meeting to go hiking together the next morning. I told them where I had camped so they could find me.

JJ and Dave came to get me in the morning. The evening before I learned that JJ worked for Amazon and I was very interested in talking with him. We had a great conversation the whole time, and I enjoyed talking with Dave, too. They were both very smart. After the hike, there was more music, and we met up with Dave's equally awesome wife, Elisa. We decided to walk around the amphitheater and area, listening to music and people watching. Before we started, Dave turned to me, "No one has pockets big enough, do you mind if I stash these," he held up a baggie full of cookies, "in your boots?"

I laughed, "Sure." I took them from him and got them situated comfortably in my boots.

At one point, a woman with gold nipples came up to us and offered to paint ours. Dave, Elisa, and JJ did theirs with purple glitter, and I got gold glitter on my eyelids. I felt how the choices I had made, both about my business and personally, had led me to this great experience. It made me feel very grateful and appreciative.

The next day we all met at a nearby winery before heading back to see more great bands. I felt so happy that I cried as the band Alabama Shakes performed. It was pure bliss. Listening to soulful music, dancing with new friends, in perfect weather and a perfect setting. Dave and I would look at each other and laugh for no reason. I know he felt my happiness and that I could feel his, too. It was one of those moments when everything good in life comes together. For the first time in my life, I felt like I had met a kindred spirit. It's so strange to feel that way after knowing someone for only two days.

It's important to understand the significance of this to me. I was (still am) beginning to connect with people on a deeper emotional level and loving it!

I said goodbye to them at the end of the night. I was sad but glad I would see them again soon in Seattle.

After a week of wandering around British Columbia and Vancouver Island, I parked my Winnebago in a parking lot five houses away from Dave and Elisa's home. During the day, I worked from Dave's co-working place or at local coffee shops.

My two friends Meredith and Jesse came in from Colorado. I picked them up from the Seattle airport, and we drove to the park near Dave's and slept there in the Winnebago. Mere, Jesse and I explored Seattle that day and drove to Portland the next morning. Several friends recommended we visit a particular dive bar in Portland, and we kept their suggestion in mind.

Arriving in Portland, we met Jesse's friend at a bar downtown. I was excited to see an old friend, Stanley, sitting a few tables away. We caught up on all that had gone on in our lives since we'd last seen each other and exchanged numbers. I mentioned the dive bar my friends had recommended.

"You're thinking about going to Casa Diablo later?" Stanley asked. "It is a bit sketchy, but if you're with the right people," he grinned at me "you'll like it." He rose from the table to leave. "If you go, let me know, and I'll join you."

A few hours later we met up with Stanley and went to this dive bar on the other side of town. We chatted with the two guys at a table next to us. One of them, John, seemed like an intelligent and nice guy. He asked if I wanted to go out to dinner with him while I was in Portland. We made plans to meet that coming Wednesday night.

The following day, Mere and I headed to the coast about 100 miles from Portland. We drove through Astoria, a fantastic place with rocks and formations creating some of the most beautiful seascapes in America.

On the hour drive to Long Beach, Washington just over the Columbia River, we went over the bridge during a gorgeous sunset. Just off the bridge, there were beach access roads. Some signs said driving was allowed on the beach but not camping. I turned to Mere, "Let's hit the beach!"

It didn't take long to realize that was a mistake. We got stuck a few feet after our wheels left the pavement. Even though on hard-packed sand, it couldn't take the weight of my RV! I was frustrated and pissed for a few seconds, but then realized, this was awesome! We were stuck in a beautiful spot, I had Wi-Fi so I could work, and we could also walk to town. So, we didn't try to get unstuck and spent a peaceful night of sleep right on the beach.

The next morning, I got out my bike and went for a beach bike ride. It was another one of those moments where I took it all in. I listened to the sounds of the wind, the waves and sea birds calling. I smelled the scent of the moist, salty sea air. I had the free time to notice and appreciate the play of wind and light on the water. I felt the natural feeling of my body's movements as it made unconscious adjustments of balancing and riding a bike on sand. As I rode along, my eyes filled with tears of joy. What a beautiful life. There I was, riding my bike on the beach, enjoying a view of the Pacific Ocean while taking a break from managing my company back in Colorado via computer.

I will cherish that moment and those memories forever. They were possible because I had made decisions that landed me there—that very spot on Earth—where my RV could get stuck in the sand!

Unfortunately, we couldn't stay there much longer. I called my roadside assistance service and explained my situation.

"I'm sorry, but we can't help you," he said firmly.

At first, I didn't think I heard them correctly. "Excuse me. Did you say you can't help me? Isn't that what 'roadside assistance' is for?"

"You chose to drive on the sand. Your policy only works for roads!" I hung up and started thinking about next steps.

"Hey!" I looked over at Meredith. She was pointing at something. "There's some guys over there, pulling a car out of the sand!" We jogged over. "Can you help us out?" They could. After they had got the car out of the sand and it was safely on its way, they came over in their truck—hooked up to the rear frame of my RV—and pulled us backward about five feet until we were on pavement again. We gave them a case of beer as a thank you and everyone was happy!

We went back to Portland where I dropped Mere off at the airport. From there I met John for dinner. We had pizza and drinks, and he told me how his dad had skipped town when he was seven. He hadn't seen or heard from him in more than 15 years and that watching his mom struggle had created an intensely strong work ethic in him and his brother. John became successful after a lot of hard work, "not luck," he explained. He had bought his mom a house, helping her just as she had supported and helped him grow up to become the man he was. He was impressed by my situation. I had told him about my business and that I was under contract to sell. Nodding his head, he had some advice for me (and I'm passing it on for others to think about, too): "Ask for equity. That's what can really pay off and enable you to continue to benefit from your efforts in launching and growing the business." He smiled. "And be sure to write about all this, your business experiences and some of what happened on your road trip." The next morning, he reminded me by text, "Equity Robin, ask for equity."

"I'm not good at negotiating," I texted him back.

Immediately he came back with, "It's not about negotiating … it's about asking for what you deserve. What you're asking—should ask for—is a fair request."

He suggested some key phrases to include in my request and then I wrote an email asking to add an equity piece to the deal. Now, here's something important: At one point, I had asked my broker if I should ask for equity. He discouraged it because it would make the deal more complicated and his goal was to close the transaction. Because of John's advice and prompting, without discussing it with the broker, I asked the buyer for some equity, and they accepted! Big lesson learned: You don't get if you don't ask, and sometimes you must ask several sources until you ask the right person. It was awesome that I learned this lesson—and retained a nice chunk of equity in my business—because I met a random guy at a sleazy bar! Good advice can come from the most unexpected places. I was beginning to fully understand something that Henry Ford said: "If you always do what you've always done, you'll always get what you've always got."

From Portland, I drove to Eugene, Oregon to visit my friend Matt. A creative metalsmith, he is an unusual and fascinating guy who has done some crazy things, like riding a unicycle across the entire Pacific Crest Trail! That's something significant because the trail reaches from Canada to Mexico and is 2,659 miles long, ranges in elevation from just above sea level at the

Oregon–Washington border to 13,153 feet at Forester Pass in the Sierra Nevada and passes through 25 national forests and seven national parks. Wow! Matt and his girlfriend Sherman were preparing for the big country fair. They had volunteered to help and would ride their bikes 40 miles to the campground and camp out there for a week.

All this time, for about eight weeks, due diligence on the sale of my business had been underway. We had cleared all the details, the back and forth of the investigation, questions, and answers confirming everything in the deal. And then we were done. The same day Matt and Sherman left for the fair, the sale of my business closed! Just like that. The terms of the deal were that I would advise the private equity firm in their new ownership for six months and as part of the purchase price, keep a 7.5% stake in the business. Just as John in Portland told me, now I would always have a vested interest in its success. It was a great deal for both the buyer and for me.

I finally accomplished something I had anticipated all my life. I was a millionaire but wasn't even excited about it. The next morning, I went to another coffee shop and started training the new owner of the business and afterward, went to a salon and got my hair dyed purple. I thought that was a fun way to celebrate becoming a millionaire! Now, I was truly free to find and begin work on the 'next thing' in my life!

And part of that is to help others become inspired by not just my story but that of other entrepreneurs. This book shares several, and I'm sure that having read them you've picked up on a common thread: they all took things into their own hands. They did not ask for permission or wait until they had a solid plan. Often, they started with less than perfect circumstances, but that did not stop them. An important lesson to learn: don't wait for perfect conditions. Sometimes all you need is a small break; one you may have to create for yourself. But when you have one, you must be ready to take advantage of it. These entrepreneurs teach us something significant if you want more from life: don't wait for gatekeepers or someone's approval to create something and present it to the world. That approach has proved worthwhile for me. Maybe it will work for you, too.

> *"For what it's worth... it's never too late, or in my case too early, to be whatever you want to be. There's no time limit. Start whenever you want. You can change or stay the same. There are no rules to this thing. We can make the best or the worst of it. I hope you make the best of it. I hope you see things that startle you. I hope you feel things you never felt before. I hope you meet people who have a different point of view. I hope you live a life you're proud of, and*

if you're not, I hope you have the courage to start all over again."
— Eric Roth, screenplay writer,
The Curious Case of Benjamin Button

AFTERWORD

"Women need to shift from thinking, 'I'm not ready to do that' to thinking 'I want to do that and I'll learn by doing it.'"
—SHERYL SANDBERG

We read so much, so often, about big business and famous entrepreneurs... too many to name here. And it's okay if we choose to emulate them. But keep this in mind: for every Oprah Winfrey, Jeff Bezos of Amazon, or Steve Jobs of Apple... there's hundreds if not thousands of successful business owners around you. They're male and female... young and old, college educated or lacking a degree. No matter the type, it's almost certain they started with one thing: the desire to live life on their own terms.

Reading inspirational stories is great, but as you read them they must connect with you in some way, or they pass quickly out of mind. You must see that positive outcome—the good results achieved—as being something you too can attain. The individuals in the stories you just read are regular people who are executing their own ideas. We hope they inspire you to do the same. And that they serve as role models or examples, to help people look up, look forward and realize that they too can succeed.

We (all involved with this book) hope that these stories create a connection that helps keep you moving forward toward your goal of becoming an entrepreneur or business owner. Please remember, success can be defined in many ways. I like to think that it is doing the best you can with what you've got. You'll never know what you're capable of if you don't try.

Here's what I see as the important takeaways from the contributor's stories:

Lori Ames: Sometimes circumstances require you to change and go down a path entirely new to you and perhaps not one you've ever contemplated. Necessity—in this case, the need to care for her son—required her to start her own business and set her own professional course.

Stacey Blume: Ideas for a business or product can happen at any time and in any place. You must keep your mind open to see them and then explore which ones work and which do not. Stacey's journey exemplifies this and what the rewards can be.

Jenny Dorsey: One of the hardest things to deal with and overcome, is the disapproval of others. We tend to measure ourselves by what others think, but that is not good for us. Jenny discovered that you need to determine your value based on how you feel about yourself, about what you're doing today and what you plan to do in the future.

Carrie Hammer: What can be tougher to overcome than an industry-wide, virtually indelibly ingrained in our social psyche and consciousness, standard convention about who is beautiful and who is not. Carrie took that on from within the multi-billion-dollar Beauty & Fashion industry, working with other like-minded people and organizations, to change the perception of beauty... to make it become what it should be. She's doing that because the status quo was so truly wrong and hurts so many girls and young women's self-perception, that she could not stand aside. Her, "No, I'm not going to keep doing it their way..." has turned Carrie's business into a powerful engine helping to drive a compelling social movement.

Jody Harris: Jody's climb to where she is now, a successful professional, inventor, and business owner, proves that when things are bleak—even life-threatening—you can make decisions to change those circumstances. And you can find the strength to make your dreams a reality. Jody shows that you can turn a problem's solution into thriving business.

Cynthia Jamin: What's past... is passed. Just because you've experienced something tragic does not mean you can't have a wonderful life and build a successful business. You can create a bright future and put the past behind you to help bring beauty and joy into our world. Cynthia exemplifies this.

Erin Janklow: Sometimes in life, we encounter situations and people who think we should be something or someone other than who we are. You must be authentic, true to who you really are if you expect to be focused enough to have a good life. Erin has taken that philosophy to helping hospitality employees learn English while on the job, which helps them grow and helps the business improve... a win-win for everyone.

Ericka Michelle Lassair: Many people see it as permanent. The 'that's it... I'm done...' reaction after a setback or failure. They took a shot, missed, and they don't try again. But in truth, every person who has achieved some measure of success has failed before. Sometimes many times. Like Ericka, they were willing to learn from experience and rebuild... to start again in a different way, and better prepared the next time.

Irina Skoeries: What happens is what you make happen. Right? Some things are beyond our control, but we can determine what happens next by how we react and respond to the problem. Irina took the devastating news that her health problems would not get better and found a way to heal herself through food. That, in turn, led to her business and tremendous opportunity. Her story is a testimonial to making what happens... what you want.

Meredith Sorensen: It's always the end game that most fixate on. Reaching the objective, the destination. But Meredith's story shows that it's the journey that leads to discovery... that every step we take makes us who we are... who we become. Over time we evolve and get better at what we do. Use what you learn on the journey to help you. Meredith's journey has led to a vocation and advocacy for recycling to help conserve our world's precious resources. Every person on Earth benefits from that effort.

Stephanie Winans: Again, a lesson on how you can change things to form what works best for you. That often means taking some level of risk—a step into the unknown. Inspiration is all around us. Take what you know, learn from those around you, and as Stephanie has done, use or repurpose it in different ways to achieve what you want and need.

Dan Caldwell: Dan grew up poor, in a violent neighborhood, full of self-doubts that he could find a way to achieve what he wanted from life. Those misgivings were fueled even further by failure at becoming a police officer. But he overcame those uncertainties, took his passion for the sport of Mixed-Martial Arts (MMA), and along with two partners formed a business that became wildly successful. He moved forward with faith that he would make it if he kept trying. Making that decision and taking the first steps made all the difference between where he was then and now.

Robin Behrstock: You must take risks. Don't be afraid of what you don't know. You'll learn what you need to along the way. Get outside of your comfort zone. That can be unpleasant at first, but you need to do it to learn and grow. You should be willing to start and not let the challenges stop you. You should think differently about what success means exactly for you, and how you can accomplish it. Doing it for the money will only get you so far, and you'll get burnt out. Do something you're passionate about sharing with the world. That is what will sustain you. And don't forget... pay it forward: you should write your story for others to read and become inspired by.

Now let's take the first steps toward writing your story. Answer the questions that follow, or go to our website to answer: http://www.AWEBOOK.com/Questions.

If you use our website, you can choose to get reminder emails, and we'll check in on your story's progress at the time interval you want.

> What is something in your life you want to change or improve?

___

> What do you want to accomplish in the next year?

___

> Where do you want to be in 3 years, personally and professionally?

___

> Where do you want to be in 5 years, personally and professionally?

___

Congratulations! By writing these things down, you've taken the first step toward accomplishing them. We hope you'll continue to do whatever needs to be done to get where you want to be. Whether or not you reach your final goal, you'll be stronger and wiser from what you've learned on your journey.

ABOUT THE AUTHOR

ROBIN BEHRSTOCK

Robin has been starting businesses since she was a kid. Most of them were failures that became learning experiences. At the age of 33, it all paid off when she started a copper mug business just as they became a popular trend.

In less than three years, she grew the business to annual sales of $3MM. With that success came the realization it wasn't what she wanted to do with her life. The best part of being an entrepreneur—for her—wasn't making money or selling lots of copper mugs, it was inspiring people. Long-term, that's what she wanted to do.

This book became her new focus, with the goal of inspiring women around the world to do something different, to step outside their comfort zone or move beyond their present circumstances and make their dreams a reality.

CPSIA information can be obtained
at www.ICGtesting.com
Printed in the USA
FSOW02n0749110517
34116FS

9 780998 787008